Figures of a Changing World

HARRY BERGER, JR.

Figures of a Changing World

METAPHOR AND THE EMERGENCE
OF MODERN CULTURE

Fordham University Press
New York 2015

Fordham University Press also publishes its books in a variety of electronic formats. Some content that appears in print may not be available in electronic books.

Visit us online at www.fordhampress.com.

Library of Congress Cataloging-in-Publication Data available online at catalog.loc.gov.

Printed in the United States of America

17 16 15 5 4 3 2 1

First edition

for Helen

CONTENTS

ACKNOWLEDGMENTS

Figures of a Changing World began its existence a long time ago. I moved from New Haven to Santa Cruz in 1965, and in the next year I was joined by my former Yale colleague H. Marshall Leicester, now an eminent Chaucerian and film scholar. During that year Marsh and I used to get together almost daily to work on an essay on *Beowulf.* I remember our sitting in a room that wasn't yet furnished: no chairs or tables or couches or books. What we sat on and worked on was the carpet: a *vita nuova* in an empty room. It was then that we began worrying about the differences among tropes, or figures of speech. The basic distinctions between metaphor and metonymy that structure the present book thus took root in discussions that occurred almost a half-century ago. Though both of us have relocated several times, today we're neighbors again. Since I've been indebted to Marsh for so many things—things that transcend tropes—during the intervening years, it gives me the greatest pleasure to thank him for the light he shone then and continues to shine now on the thinking and writing and living we've done and still do together.

I decided a few years ago to try to finish the study of tropes that was initiated in my meetings with Marsh. This would have been a lot harder to do if I hadn't been blessed with other sources of assistance and support. Once again, as so often before, my wife, Beth Pittenger, suggested a number of changes that sharpened the interpretive points

I was trying to make. And once again, Tom Lay's editorial interventions were always on point. Also, throughout the final stages of revision and proofreading, my constant guide and companion was the Managing Editor of Fordham Press, Eric Newman. His patience and encouragement and suggestions helped me get through some gnarly editorial crises and cruxes. I'm very grateful to Eric for all his help. I'm also deeply grateful to Teresa Jesionowski and Lauren Schufran: to Teresa for her wonderful editorial preparation of the manuscript and to Lauren for creating an index that not only makes me want to read the book again but also reveals connections I wasn't aware I had made.

I dedicate this book to the memory of Helen Tartar. Helen and I go back a long way. We worked together for sixteen years, seven at Stanford University Press and nine at Fordham University Press. Helen encouraged me to submit the manuscript of *The Fictions of the Pose* to Stanford Press when I had just about given up on it. As humanities editor, she oversaw its production. Acting at the same time as copy editor, she suggested an embarrassingly large number of revisions—major and minor, conceptual and technical—that substantially strengthened both the style of the book and its argument. Without Helen's supervision, without her participation at every level and phase of production, *Fictions of the Pose* would never have gotten off the ground. It wasn't only that she had such a complete purchase on what I had done and needed to do. It was also that she had a special gift of restrained communication: She would drop hints and cues that left it up to me to decide what to do with passages that needed revision.

Her remarkable powers of discrimination, her breadth of knowledge, her generosity of spirit couldn't possibly be contained in her official press titles. Poet, scholar, critic, and philosopher, she would be the exemplary editor were she not unique and therefore inimitable. Her patience, her openness to new ideas, her critical sensibility, and above all her willingness to Just Say No kept me from both writing too much and not writing at all.

Very early in our relationship I began to rely on Helen's capacious understanding of current discourses in the humanities and social sciences, and on her unerring sense of what is to be valued in such discourses. Because my own work transgresses discursive boundaries, it was absolutely vital for me to have a colleague who knew enough about these areas to keep me honest and curb my enthusiasm.

My life as an academic writer has been so deeply interinvolved with and dependent on Helen Tartar's editorial genius for so many years that I now feel there's little reason to continue in that life. Helen was not only my dream editor. She was my pal, my teacher, my sister. She combined openness, warmth, and receptivity with the world's most judicious and farsighted critical sensibility. Her attentiveness to the details of literary, expository, and rhetorical form became my touchstone. Whatever I wrote and still write, I wrote and still write for Helen and to Helen, and this will not change during the remainder of my writing life.

Helen has gone, but her voice reverberates in the shadows of my mind as she knits away and we chat away and she looks up and laughs away.

Mind over matter is matter undermined.

—Old saying

PART I

Theory and Practice

ONE

Two Figures: (1) Metaphor

I begin with an absolutely arbitrary and unwarranted assertion, namely, that given a distinction between metaphor and metonymy, the tendency to make metaphors is characteristic of the modern attitude, while the tendency to see metonymies is characteristic of the traditional attitude. Any traditional ambience that becomes a cosmos does so because it has been structured into a field for the perception of metonymies, has been organized, we might say, by the metonymizing process. Modernization (or disenchantment) is then the transformation of metonymies into metaphors; to modernize is to de-metonymize, to metaphorize. To re-traditionalize is to de-metaphorize, to re-metonymize. The traditional attitude privileges the metonymizing process; the modern attitude privileges the metaphorizing process.

The trouble with such assertions is not so much that they seem arbitrary, as that they seem incomprehensible, so freighted down with jargon as to inhibit any rapid transit of meaning from writer to reader. Besides, who needs another account of metaphor and metonymy, which have already been the victims of vigorous overelaboration in linguistic and semiotic circles, not to mention hermeneutic circles? These accounts, however, have indeed stayed in orbit and retained their equidistance from the central point to be developed in the following discussion. The difference between metaphor and metonymy is the difference between making and seeing: making metaphors, but seeing metonymies. On the one hand, a metaphor is something we make; it wasn't there before we made it; we brought it into being. On the other hand, a metonymy is something we see; we didn't make it up; it was already there.

We all know that a metaphor is a figure comparing two things without the use of "like" or "as," a transfer of terms from their proper or literal signification that is grammatically phrased as an assertion of identity. Consider two famous examples, "Achilles is a lion" and "my love is a rose," the first immortalized by Homer, the second by centuries of sexist discourse.[1] Both display

> the tripartite structure of all metaphors, often stressed by theoreticians of rhetoric. When Homer calls Achilles a lion, the literal meaning of the figure signifies an animal of a yellowish brown color, living in Africa, having a mane, etc. The figural meaning signifies Achilles and the proper meaning the attribute of courage or strength that Achilles and the lion have in common and can therefore exchange.[2]

De Man's analysis makes it clear that of the three meanings the literal is most likely to invite readers to conjure up a visual image, and my point about this is that the visual image then gets put under erasure in the dynamic transition to the figural and proper senses.

It's important to appreciate the dynamic and countervisual properties of metaphor. Nobody thinks Achilles is or actually looks like a lion. Nobody thinks the poet who says "my love is a rose" means "I'm in love with roses" rather than "the person I love is a rose" (she isn't, really) or "my affection is a rose" (it isn't, really).[3] The transfer affects the thing referred to and the verbal reference together, and here the effect is apiary: Whenever the male poet deposits the properties of a rose on the referent of "my love," the properties of his love are temporarily visited on the flowery referent of "a rose."

Again, no one familiar with that figure takes it as a cue to visualization. We aren't motivated to picture the beloved wearing petals or bearing thorns. So conspicuously absurd a possibility reminds us that if a figure recognized as metaphor initially feints toward visualization of the things its terms refer to, it does so only to force us beyond visualization and toward interpretation. Any attempt to visualize a metaphor produces a grotesque image, a monster, especially when the opposition is sharpened to the point of catachresis.[4] As the syntagmatic order of de Man's comment shows, metaphor demands that its images be dissolved into or reconstructed as meanings. But the effect of countervisuality depends on and presupposes a feint toward the visualizable.

A is B / A is not B: This is the conceptual structure of metaphor, and although most of my isolated examples tend to reflect it, we should keep in mind the difference between a trope's conceptual structure and its grammatical form—a difference that has been brilliantly explored by Christine Brooke-Rose in *A Grammar of Metaphor*.[5] Drawing her examples from the works of fifteen English poets and adopting the simplest of definitions—metaphor "is any replacement of one word by another, or any identification of one thing, concept or person with any other" (23–24)—she examines the differences produced by different types of grammatical linkage.[6]

The grammatical variability on which Brooke-Rose's study centers belongs to the surface structure of metaphor but, as her definition indicates, it also has an invariant deep structure, which is pseudo-propositional and duplex in form. It consists of an identity assertion,

"A is B," coupled with its implied contradictory, "A is not B." The exclusion of the simile's "like" or "as" serves to sharpen the collision between A and B, especially when the context seems to support a strong or existential rather than a weak or predicative sense of "is."[7] I note in passing that metaphoric propositions needn't be reversible. "A rose is my love": This is less likely to be taken as a poetic inversion than as a straightforward if melodramatically reticent expression of anthophilia.[8]

A more homespun way to phrase the oppositional deep structure is "A is B, but not really." "What matters," as Donald Davidson insists,

> is not actual falsehood but that the sentence be taken to be false. . . . Generally it is only when a sentence is taken to be false that we accept it as a metaphor and start to hunt out the hidden implication. It is probably for this reason that most metaphorical sentences are patently false. . . . Absurdity or contradiction in a metaphorical sentence guarantees we won't believe it and invites us, under proper circumstances, to take the sentence metaphorically.[9]

The intensity of the opposition is what pumps a metaphor up and lets it take off; as the negative becomes weaker through use, the metaphor suffers deflation and loses altitude until it is grounded in literalness.

Such phrases as "the leg of the table" or "the mouth of the bottle" are no longer bizarre when visualized because both "leg" and "mouth" have left their bodily origins behind and now designate more general functions of support and ingress.[10] We view the identity assertion as conspicuously imaginary or counterfactual only as long as we feel the pressure of the negation. Metaphor denies actual or preexisting states of affairs, rejects distinctions taken for granted in normal usage, yokes together items that belong in different contexts, different "worlds" or frames of reference.

What a living metaphor asserts, reveals, or creates is therefore generated by and confined within the particular linguistic utterance that gives rise to it and that contextually sustains or reinforces the negation.[11] It is like a hapax legomenon, a nonce usage, and it therefore demands to be interpreted. All this indicates the obvious, which is that *use* matters. To repeat Davidson's emphasis, "Metaphor belongs exclusively to the domain of use. It is something brought off by the imaginative employment of words and sentences" (247).

"A is B, but not really": The version of metaphor characterized by this formula differs from—and needs to be protected from—the versions featured by George Lakoff and Mark Johnson in *Metaphors We Live By* and *Philosophy in the Flesh*. Lakoff and Johnson insist that the traditional tendency to treat metaphor exclusively within the boundaries of poetry, rhetoric, and language has been misguided. Metaphor is not merely a rhetorical trope or linguistic entity but a concept and a cognitive function. They focus on the pervasiveness and systematicity of the metaphorical concepts by which we understand and experience "one kind of thing in terms of another."[12]

Lakoff and Johnson are careful to define metaphor in a manner that emphasizes things (concepts) rather than words: "The essence of metaphor is understanding and experiencing one kind of thing in terms of another."[13] Thus in the metaphors "argument is war," "time is money," "a purposeful life is a journey," and "love is a journey," the equation is not between the terms "argument," "war," "love," "journey," and so on, but between the domains of activity and discourse those terms designate.[14] These conceptual "mappings" govern our common understanding of argument and time. They "structure our actions and thoughts," and they so permeate everyday thought and language as to render them largely imperceptible to their users. Nevertheless, it is misleading to refer to them as "dead" metaphors. "They are 'alive' in the most fundamental sense: they are metaphors we live by. The fact that they are conventionally fixed within the lexicon of English makes them no less alive" (55).[15]

For my purposes, the most significant moves made by Lakoff and his associates are their elaboration of the category of conventional metaphor, their disconnecting it from the category of dead metaphor, and their insistence that conventional metaphors like those mentioned above operate at the level of "the cognitive unconscious": "Such general metaphors as A LIFETIME IS A DAY . . . are conceptual, not linguistic, in nature, and . . . have the form of structural mappings across conceptual domains."[16] These mappings are called *metaphor* "because they are . . . responsible for the phenomenon traditionally called metaphor. . . . Metaphorical language . . . is the language that conventionally expresses the source-domain concept of a conceptual metaphor. Thus . . . the conceptual metaphor A LIFETIME IS A DAY . . . maps twilight onto old age and night onto death." In this way, "conventional metaphorical language is simply a consequence of the existence of conventional metaphorical thought."[17]

Important as this introduction of the category of conventional metaphor is, it leaves open the question whether live conventional metaphors exhibit the formula "A is B, but not really."[18] The answer is that if, in the Lakoff/Johnson/Turner system, the element of negation is taken into account, it plays a minor role and is mentioned only in casual reminders that in any metaphor the overlap between A and B is never total, always partial.[19] Despite a lot of rhetorical muscle-flexing in their attack on traditional views of metaphor, their complex and exhaustively worked-out theory produces an account of metaphor that reduces it functionally to the status of a simile: not "A is B, but not really" but "A is [like] B," "A resembles B in certain respects."

Consider a representative sample of the conceptual metaphors on their list:

A. "Target domain"		B. "Source domain"
Love	is	a journey[20]
Life	is	a journey
Death	is	departure
People	are	plants
Death	is	rest
Life	is	a flame[21]

However variously Lakoff, Johnson, and Turner describe the relations between these domains, they define "a mapping" as the actualization of "a set of correspondences."[22] Although they are careful to argue against notions that metaphors express preexisting, literal, or symmetrical similarities not based on cross-domain mapping, their account of mapping is nothing if not a definition of metaphor in terms of resemblance or similarity: "The conventional Love is a Journey metaphor creates a . . . Love is a Journey concept, which of course has similarities to journeys—exactly the similarities expressed in the mapping, since the mapping creates the similarities."[23]

A theory of metaphor that bases itself on the formula, "A is B, but not really," can't be reduced to or equated with the view of conventional metaphor as cross-domain mapping, the basic formula of which is closer to that of simile: "A is [like] B." Simile is a positive analogy, metaphor a negative one. Or, as Davidson puts it, "The most obvious semantic difference between simile and metaphor is that all similes are true and most metaphors are false."[24] What Lakoff, Johnson, and Turner call "metaphor" appears in my scheme as a metaphoric simile. From now on, therefore, I'll distinguish their concept from mine by designating theirs as *weak* and mine as *strong* metaphor.[25] The qualitative sense of the distinction is concisely expressed in Davidson's varied repetition of the statement quoted above: "Most metaphorical sentences are *patently* false, just as all similes are trivially true," which also says something about the Lakoff/Johnson/Turner reduction of metaphor to metaphoric simile.[26]

TWO

Two Figures: (2) Metonymy

Metaphora is a Greek term precipitated from the verb *metapherein*, to carry something from one place to another—a sense acknowledged early in the twentieth century when I. A. Richards gave the name "vehicle" to the predicating term of a metaphor.[1] But the initial context of vehiculation is more pragmatic than poetic. *Metapherein* means—switching now from Greek *meta* to Latin *trans*—"to transfer" (as of property) or "to transport" (as in the hauling of goods).[2] Transferred to the *techné* and *logos* of rhetorical discourse, the noun means "transfer of a word to a new sense."

The rhetorical meaning of *metaphora* is thus a metaphorical extension of legal and commercial meanings. In rhetoric, any term that enters into a metaphoric negotiation undergoes a shift of semantic burden. This reminds us that metaphor, however poetic and airy a view we take of it, carries the markings of the home base from which it deviates, the base still quaintly—metaphorically—characterized as *oikonomia* (rules of the house; domestic order). *Oikonomia* designates a system of rules and the practices of exchange the system organizes: exchanges between or among genders, generations, families, households, lineages, communities, tribes, corporate groups, institutions, and nations. The economics of metaphor can't avoid being implicated in the metaphorics of economy—or should I say, the metonymics of economy?

The word *metonymy* comes from Greek *metonomasia* (Latin *metonymia*), "a change of name," and the action it designates involves moving or extending a name from one referent to another: "Sail" is extended to the referent of "ship"; the name of a material, "marble," is extended to the referent of "a statue" made of the material; the traditional name of a species, "man," is extended to the referents of "women and children," who belong to the species. It may or may not be important that the root term, *onoma*, means "name," not "word" (*logos* or *lexis*). The relations of metonymy are various modes of contiguity and association: between whole and part, container and contained, sign and thing signified, material and thing made, cause and effect, genus and species.[3]

Most dictionary definitions are less laconic than the one in Liddell and Scott's *Greek–English Lexicon*: "metonomasia, change of name." They include one or more of the various modes of contiguity and association listed above: "the substitution of the name of an object for that of another to which it has some relation, as the name of the cause for that of the effect, of the property for that of the substance, etc.; a metonymy" (Lewis and Short's *Latin Dictionary*);[4] "a figure of speech which consists of substituting for the name of a thing the name of an attribute of it or of something closely related" (*OED*); "a figure of speech consisting of the use of the name of one thing for that of another of which it is an attribute or with which it is associated (as 'crown' in 'lands belonging to the crown')" (*Merriam-Webster's Collegiate Dictionary, Eleventh Edition*). *The American Heritage Dictionary* (third edition) differs in not using the word "name": "a figure of speech in which one word or phrase is substituted for another with which it is closely associated, as in the use of Washington for the United States government." Notice, however, that "Washington" and "United States" are proper nouns, and proper nouns differ from common nouns in designating individual referents rather than such generic referents as "a rose" or "beloved." Washington may be substituted for the United States government because it is already associated with it by forms of contiguity (part/whole, container/contained) in the real world.[5]

In the present study I argue that metaphors involve modifications of meaning produced by the rhetorical context, whereas metonymies involve analytic or descriptive changes of name that may illuminate but don't change the prior meanings of the things signified. Metaphors rhetorically challenge the similarity they grammatically claim to establish, in order to feature their departures from preexisting states of affairs. Metonymies present themselves as analogies that articulate or reaffirm preexisting states of affairs. They are guarantors of *facticity,* a term that can be translated or defined as *fact-like-ness.*

Unlike fact and factuality, facticity names a state of appearance and resemblance and thus implies a rhetorical effect, a trope. By an imaginative employment of false etymology we can link it to *factitious* as to its adjective. *Factitious* means artificially produced and therefore lacking authenticity: fake, sham. *Factitious* slides easily, by a one-letter change, into *fictitious. Factitious* also shares a common etymology with *fetish, fetishistic*—both derive (the latter via Portuguese) from Latin *facticius.* To fetishize is to confer an especially intense degree of facticity as a repository and guarantor of value; to characterize the conferral as fetishizing is to affirm that it is factitious or fictitious. Given a context of competing ideological economies, the production of facticity depends on the development and maintenance of strategies of defictionalization. Metonymizing is such a strategy, whereas metaphorizing is a strategy of fictionalization.[6]

On the basis of this distinction I go on to argue that metaphor and metonymy can be used as instruments both for the macrointerpretation of tensions in culture change and for the microinterpretation of tensions within particular texts. At the same time, I also suggest that the difference between the two figures can't be upheld without introducing an additional set of terms that subject the difference to historical or cultural determination. And this poses a problem. For how can metaphor and metonymy be used to interpret the very process necessary to distinguish and interpret them? I'm not sure I can solve that problem, I'm not even sure it's important from the standpoint of interpretation, but I think we have to keep it in mind to guarantee the provisional and inconclusive character of any inquiry such as this.

THREE

Making Metaphors, Seeing Metonymies

My way of formulating the contrast between metaphor and metonymy is indebted to various linguistic, structuralist, and semiotic discussions for some, but not all, of its elements. I have selectively synthesized certain aspects that characteristically emerge in those discussions and rejected others, so as to shift the emphasis of the distinction toward my focus on the problematics of culture change. Ever since Roman Jakobson placed the opposition between metaphor and metonymy at the foundations of language use, the terms have been subject to continuous definitional torquing and distension.[1] And although the privileged status of these tropes has been accepted or reinforced in the work of many rhetoricians, linguists, semioticians, and commentators on Lacanian psychoanalysis, many other writers have questioned the arbitrariness of the classification and offered competing alternatives.[2]

I won't be concerned with the career of this discussion, in part because I find debates over classification of no help in understanding the functions and effects of particular figurative contexts, in part because my interest here is only in a particular theme: the ideological implications of two relationships between rhetoric and "reality" that appear fundamentally opposed. This theme flickers in and out of many treatments of metaphor and metonymy, where it is often present in blurred form or is ancillary to the focus on classification. I'll scan a few of these, and discuss others, in order to foreground my own theme and give it sharper definition.

From Jakobson's influential discussion, modified by Christian Metz's critique, I single out four notions for further development:

1. The idea that all tropes can be subsumed under these two, which stand in opposition to each other as "two basic modes of relation." Metaphor is fundamentally paradigmatic and expresses internal relations of similarity, contrast, selection, and substitution. Metonymy is fundamentally syntagmatic and expresses external relations of combination and contiguity. After observing that Jakobson borrows the foregoing lists of attributes from structural linguistics and projects them onto "the territory of rhetoric," Metz goes on to argue that "the influence of structural linguistics, with its account of the paradigm, and the resonances which belong to it"—similarity and substitution—leads Jakobson to demote "the principle of contrast" to "merely one of the forms of similarity."[3] He therefore proposes to substitute "comparability" for "similarity" (188). In view of the distinction I make above between weak and strong metaphor, I want to insist that even "comparability" is too weak—that contrast and tension between the terms being "compared" are primary features of metaphor.[4]

2. The idea that metonymic relationships involve, and often confuse, different kinds of contiguity (linguistic, temporal or narrative, spatial, and causal). Finding in Jakobson an occasional tendency to reduce contiguity to adjacency, Metz reminds us that it involves "far more than spatial proximity" (*IS*, 188). This topic will be pursued in the discussion of Nietzsche that occupies the next section.

3. The association of metaphor with poetry and symbolism, and of metonymy with prose and realism. According to Claude Lévi-Strauss, for example, a fundamental "law of mythical thought" is "that the transformation of a metaphor is achieved in a metonymy," by which he means that something fictional—purely figurative—is transformed into something taken for real.[5] Metz brings out the significance of this distinction both more fully and more suggestively than Jakobson when, after warning against the dangerous imprecision it encourages (195), he comments on a dissymmetry between the two tropes:

> The metonymic act is inherently more probable, and almost certainly more frequent, than the metaphorical act. . . . [Metonymic] contiguity is a "real" connection (felt to be real), and [metaphoric] resemblance a "felt" connection (felt to be felt). Which no doubt explains all those fashionable generalizations about metaphorical creativity and metonymic prosaicism. . . . Stephen Ullmann [remarks the dissymmetry when he states] . . . that connections based on contiguity . . . are "given" or "external"; those based on resemblance are never more than "latent" in things, they always have to be partly "invented." (202–3)

The oppositions poetry/prose, symbolic/realistic, and invented/given are themselves varied metonymic incidences of the global contrast the present essay aims both to construct and to deconstruct.

4. The emphasis on metonymizing and metaphorizing as processes and "acts." For my purposes, this is the most important of the four notions. The context of Jakobson's discussion is a pair of essays in which he tries to establish the usefulness of his brand of linguistics to the diagnosis of speech disorders. His primary concern is therefore with participation in speech events, patterns of verbal communication, and constraints on the agency of the speaker. Metz diverts the structural dynamism of this approach via Freud toward Lacan's revision of Jakobson: When "Lacan tells us that the unconscious is structured like

a language, he brings condensation and displacement into line with metaphor and metonymy" (*IS*, 229), thus reassigning them from dream-work and primary process to the symbolic order of language, where they reappear as the "chief 'figurations'" of that order (153, 168–69).

In Freudian theory both processes are expressly depicted as motivated fantasy constructions; displacement may depend on previously experienced contiguities whereas condensation may fuse previously experienced disparities, but the difference between the two processes is formal rather than ontological. To assimilate the rhetorical to the psychological processes is to obscure the epistemic difference between making and seeing, and between their correlative forms of language use, the creative force of metaphorizing and the mimetic force of metonymizing.[6] This can't be thought of as a rigid distinction because it is not inherent in the order of the signifier per se but results from a difference produced by discursive practices that construct or construe strong or creative metaphor as a hapax legomenon.

The general tendency in the theory and study, and especially in the classification, of metaphor and metonymy is nevertheless to accentuate the structural distinction between the two tropes, and—under the influence first of Saussure's structural linguistics and then of Jakobson's—to do so in terms of linguistic rather than rhetorical categories. Some writers treat metaphor as more daring or inventive and metonymy as more prosaic. Paul Ricoeur, for example, entertains the idea that metaphor involves modification of meaning while metonymy is limited to the substitution of names. Umberto Eco, to whose work I return below, argues that whereas metonymy reflects the existing segmentation of cultural content by the linguistic code, metaphor in various ways segments "the substance of content to the point of transforming it into a new form of content."[7] Others, like Claude Lévi-Strauss in the passage cited above, focus on transformational possibilities. Still others argue about whether a particular figure is metaphor or metonymy, or whether there are cases of intersection or ambivalence or oscillation.[8]

What these notions have in common is brought out in Edmund Leach's recapitulation of previous accounts of the distinction. Leach contrasts two subclasses of the basic category of "signum": (1) "A signum is a sign when there is intrinsic prior relationship between A and B because they belong to the same cultural context." For example, "given the context of European political traditions in which the principal item of the ruling monarch's regalia was a crown, a crown is a sign for sovereignty." In this metonymic relationship, "the index which functions as a sign is contiguous to and part of that which is signified," and Leach adds that "natural indices (e.g., 'smoke indicates fire') entail metonymic relationships as well as signs." (2) A "signum is a symbol when A stands for B and there is no intrinsic prior relationship between A and B, that is to say, A and B belong to different cultural contexts." For example, "where a crown is used as a trademark for a brand of beer, it is a symbol not a sign. There is no prior intrinsic relationship. Crowns and beer come from different contexts." Leach concludes that "the contrast between the intrinsic relationships entailed in natural indices and [cultural] signs and the non-intrinsic relationships entailed in symbols corresponds to the distinction between metonymy and metaphor. Where metonymy implies contiguity, metaphor depends upon asserted similarity."[9] Although the terms of Leach's contrast are clear, the sharpness of the distinction between intrinsic and nonintrinsic forms is muddied by his particular example, for once the crown is contextually fixed and repetitively displayed as a trademark, it ceases to be a hapax legomenon and enters into an emblematic or metonymic relation with the enterprise it signifies.

It seems clear that if the distinction between intrinsic and nonintrinsic relationships is made criterial, the various forms those relationships can take becomes a secondary consideration. This is why such classificational questions as those concerning the difference, say, between metonymy and synecdoche diminish in importance. From the standpoint of an interest in classification, Gérard Genette may well be justified in his impatience with the tendency to privilege the polarity of what he calls "the irreplaceable bookends of . . . modern rhetoric." Genette criticizes the "reduction of the figures of 'connection' to the single model of spatial metonymy" and the corresponding reduction of "the figures of 'resemblance'" to metaphor. While arguing for a more flexible attitude toward the range and diversity of figures of analogy, he also counsels against the overvaluation of analogical relations at the expense of other features of general rhetoric.[10] But apart from the fact that Genette's emphasis on resemblance slights the more fundamental contribution of difference to the impact of metaphor, the alignment of "connection" with intrinsic relationships and of "resemblance/difference" with nonintrinsic relationships is what makes the bookends irreplaceable. If, however, we shift attention from the select library of modern rhetoric and structuralism to the more vulgar confines of dictionaries and textbooks, do we find that the library distinctions recapitulated by Leach get any support from that quarter?

What we find is that textbook accounts of metaphor reduce it to weak metaphor, that is, they tend to overstress the elements of similarity, resemblance, or identity. Consider some examples: My love is a rose; my love is a moth; the gurgling voice of the waterfall; his stomach talks incessantly; the pig spilled his soup on the table; my neighbor is an elephant; the elephant is helping me pack my trunk. Confronted by such instances, the textbooks presuppose a difference between the two things placed in relation by the transfer of names (the difference, for example, between my love and a moth), and they focus on the way metaphor overcomes the difference. But we can learn more about metaphor if we focus on the overcoming of that overcoming—that is, if we see metaphor as bringing the difference before us through the pretense of overcoming it. So William Empson writes that in a living (as opposed to a dead) metaphor we recognize "that 'false identity' is being used" and feel "'resistance' to it"; and this is "rather like going into higher gear, because the machinery of interpretation must be brought into play."[11] Something has been asserted that is not the case, and we are challenged to explore the ways in which it might make sense at some other level.

Metaphor is Art, and *Webster's Dictionary of Synonyms* accordingly finds it devious, therefore imaginative: It "differs from simile in not stating explicitly that it is an analogy; it therefore imaginatively identifies one object with another, and ascribes to the first one or more of the qualities of the second, or invests the former with emotional or imaginative associations attached to the latter."[12] Even weak metaphor is too strange and dangerous for *Webster's* to get close enough to classify, but it finds metonymy (and synecdoche) comfortably *heimlich*, an appropriate and docile object for taxonomic science. It is easy to sort out the ways "in which the name of one thing is given for that of another which bears a close relationship to the first thing."[13] Metonymy embraces and accentuates the kinship of things where metaphor traffics in deviance.

As some of the illustrations and categories in *Webster's* clearly show, metonymy does not cultivate the metaphoric negation:

> "the pen is mightier than the sword" (sign for thing signified)
> "the kettle is boiling" (container for contained)
> "to read Dante" (cause for effect—Dante for his poems)
> "all hands were put to work" (part for whole)
> "one of the finest marbles in the exhibition" (material for things made from the material)

We can compare these with metaphor by rewriting them as two-place predicates: "The pen is a weapon"; "the kettle is water"; "Dante is his poem(s)"; "the hands are the man"; "the statue is a (piece of) marble." Do we feel the pressure of false identity that draws the negation? The first example is of course subject to ideological interference: A military person might wish to argue that the assertion, if not the figure, is untrue; but he would probably have to use the pen to do it, thereby proving its force as a weapon. In addition, the figure is metonymically overdetermined. "The pen" can name the part that replaces several wholes (writers, writing, medium of communication), or it can name the cause that replaces the effect (writing, etc., substituted for literary power). The metaphoric "A is B" form thus condenses several metonymic chains of preexisting associations, and this diminishes the force of "A is not B." I note in passing, however, that if someone in early sixth-century Athens said, "The stylus is a sword," the sharp edge of negation would cut more deeply into the statement; and if he wrote it, not many people would read it, either to themselves or to each other.

In the second example, the transfer of names from water to kettle is motivated by an already existing relation of container to contained, and by the knowledge that the kettle and heat together are required to make the water within it boil. If we construe the hot kettle as cause and the boiling water as effect, then "the kettle boils" reverses the causal relation. The substitution of cause for effect is one of the exchanges most often associated with the trope of metonymy. Of course, "the water boils" is no less figurative than "the kettle boils." Both are parts of a whole. The metonymy condenses a prior and more analytical account; it elliptically indicates a number of contiguous and interacting substances and functions belonging to a single process. The context reduces the force of the negation and thus turns off metaphoricity. Again, however, I note that the context is subject to a certain condition: It presupposes a smattering of lay science.

Similar explanations can be made for the last three examples, though each of them implicates ideological issues. Do we really read Dante when we read his poems? Is a man reducible to his hands? Is a work of art reducible to its material nature? The force of the negation to some extent depends on the way such questions are resolved. In general, though, all these transfers or conversions are based on

Leach's "intrinsic prior relationships"—on a prelinguistic relation between the things to which the terms refer. Unlike metaphor, the examples do not force together things that are distinct in reality, or that come from different contexts.

The terms coupled by metaphor—"my love is a rose," "John is a pig"—remind us by their syntactical proximity to each other of the very different "worlds" from which they come. Their force derives from their patently fictive coupling. They are theatrical in their self-importance. I know that John is not a pig. He shouldn't behave like one. It offends ontology: The human world differs from the animal world. It offends taste: A home is not a barn. It offends ethics: One expects more from John than from a pig.[14]

Metonymic couplings are neither so patently fictive nor so melodramatic. Marble and statue, pen and literary power, kettle and water—the two terms of each pair belong to the same context. In its most general sense, then, a metonymy is any transfer of names based on, and expressing, relationships that exist before they enter linguistic form. By its piquant expression, the form may emphasize certain aspects of the relationship, but it reflects, it doesn't reject, the contiguity or association that is the basis of that relationship.

What holds for metonymy also holds for other kinds of preexisting analogies. A person traveling through England with a map thinks, or hopes, "This map of England is like England." The expression has the form of a simile, but it is a simile in fact rather than in word, since map and England already exist in actuality as a pair related by some kind of similarity. We usually reserve the term *simile* for a situation more like that of metaphor—a particular grammatical or rhetorical formula in which analogies between the objects mentioned are produced by means of that formula and in the act of asserting likeness.

To put it in mentalist terms, metaphor in proclaiming its fictiveness pits the mind against the actual world, presents itself as the verbal dramatization of an act of consciousness seeing or creating things anew. But metonymy is a device for articulating, emphasizing, or sharpening our focus on existing interconnections and correspondences. Metonymy can help us discover, or rediscover, the one in the many, or the many within the one. But metonymy is more prosaic, modest, and reliable than metaphor, and when it connects two things that are temporally or spatially contiguous, it respects their discontinuity, their contingency.

Metonymy works within one world, and that world, preexisting and familiar, is actual, complex, and unified (though I note in passing that "actual"—that is, the appearance of actuality—designates the operative determinant of metonymic status). But metaphor works between worlds that are different from each other; it momentarily joins them in the fragile and counterfactual synthesis of a "new world."[15] This is what I meant at the beginning of this study, when I asserted that the difference between metaphor and metonymy is the difference between making and seeing—that a metaphor is something we make, something that wasn't there before we made it, whereas a metonymy is something we see, which is to say we didn't make it up; it was already there. As Susan Stewart has pointed out to me, "seeing" validates the illusion of the taken-for-grantedness that metonymy shares with dead metaphors.[16]

So much, then, we can gather by unpacking the educated lay view of the distinction from dictionaries and handbooks. But problems and possible qualifications lurk in the account, and we still have to examine the claim that the differences between metaphor and metonymy may be trivial. I argue above that the central difference concerns their relationship to actuality, existing states of affairs, "the real world," and so on. The two tropes negotiate the boundary between linguistic activity and extralinguistic reality in different ways, but to say this is to presuppose the foundational character of that boundary. I now want to test the argument against two versions of a perspective that puts pressure on the difference by questioning this presupposition. The first version is Nietzsche's, which I approach via Paul de Man, and the second is Umberto Eco's. In their very different ways and projects, both Nietzsche and Eco argue that the segmentation of the perceptual field into objects presupposes linguistic and cultural coding. Nietzsche's emphasis is on the rhetorical, Eco's on the semiotic, articulation of that field.

FOUR

Metonymy, Metaphor, and Perception: De Man and Nietzsche

In *Allegories of Reading,* Paul de Man examines Nietzsche's method of submitting "the epistemological authority of perception," language, and logic to a radically skeptical critique. Although Nietzsche was not the first to propose "that the paradigmatic structure of language is rhetorical rather than representational," he affirmed more categorically than his predecessors that "the misrepresentation of reality . . . [that he finds] systematically repeated throughout the tradition is . . . rooted in the rhetorical structure of language": "The trope is not a derived, marginal, or aberrant form of language but the linguistic paradigm par excellence. The figurative structure is not one linguistic mode among others but it characterizes language as such."[1]

There may be more to Nietzsche's critique than de Man picks out in these chapters, however, because their primary objective is not exposition of Nietzsche's theories. Their objective is to perform a rhetorical reading of the way the performativity of the text presenting Nietzsche's theories upends its constative delivery of those theories. De Man's three chapters on Nietzsche demonstrate how *The Birth of Tragedy* and other texts deconstruct themselves by deploying "a rhetorical praxis" that puts into question their "metalinguistic statements about the rhetorical nature of language."[2]

This account follows three chapters that feature discussions in which de Man contrasts metaphor and metonymy more or less after the fashion of Jakobson, Genette, and others—paradigmatic versus syntagmatic, selection versus combination, analogy versus contiguity, poetic versus prosaic. But the contrast is set up only to be interrogated, as he goes on to explore in some depth the tropological acrobatics of Marcel Proust's transgressive play with the two figures. De Man pays special attention to the divided allegiance and practice of a text in which the express preference for metaphor can't seem to prevent the poetry of its metaphors from dissolving into the prose of metonymy.[3] But nothing in this discussion prepares his reader to understand the meaning of the claim, articulated in the concluding sentence of the first Nietzsche chapter, that when *The Birth of Tragedy* is deconstructed in the manner described above, "metaphor becomes a blind metonymy."[4]

This is the first time "metonymy" is mentioned in connection with Nietzsche, and it seems to be a deliberately arcane usage. What is a metonymy that can't "see"?—can't see either the world or itself? Is "blind metonymy" a redundant phrase? In other words, is blindness to itself and its world part of the definition of metonymy? What sense can be gleaned from an outline of the interpretation that motivates de Man's claim?

De Man argues that the narrative of *The Birth of Tragedy* "acquires two incompatible narrators" (98) whose credibility the text undermines, thereby putting into question its basic representational scheme of binary oppositions:

Apollo	Dionysos
image/effect	original/cause
representation	presence
empirical reality	Being
appearance	essence, *Ding an sich*
dream, light, color	darkness
language, images	music
metaphorical figures	what metaphors mean

In what de Man calls the "genetic" interpretation, the polarity is asymmetrical. Apollo's world of illusion derives from and represents—and yet conceals—the truth of Dionysos. Dionysian being is the essence and cause, Apollonian representation its heteromorphic appearance and effect, the "metaphorical statement of this truth. The actual meaning of the Apollonian appearance is not the empirical reality it represents but the Dionysian insight into the illusory quality of this reality."[5]

A is B, but not really: In this genetic interpretation, the structure of metaphor is the paradigm of the relation between the Apollonian sign and its Dionysian referent. The metaphor "is not 'really' the [empirical] entity it literally means but it can be understood to refer to something in which meaning and being coincide." Even though it "does not mean what it says . . . , it says what it means to say, since it remains controlled by and oriented toward a specific meaning or set of meanings. Such a concept of metaphor coincides with the very notion of language conceived as a symbolic system."[6]

According to de Man, this genetic view of *The Birth of Tragedy* is wrong. It derives from a "thematic," or insufficiently rhetorical, reading. To borrow a phrase he uses in his account of Proust, it betrays "a reader caught in naive metaphorical mystification" (16). In "the rhetorically self-conscious reading" (102)—that is, the genealogical or deconstructive as opposed to the genetic reading—the Dionysian position and the asymmetrical scheme that privileges it are convincingly discredited by the Apollonian spokesman. Since the scheme is a representation, it is therefore itself an Apollonian illusion.[7] Such a "'deconstruction' of the Dionysian authority," which unfolds "within the text itself" and is confirmed by "unpublished fragments," denies the possibility that "Dionysos can enter into a world of appearances" by means of "the metaphorical narrative . . . and still remain Dionysos" (98, 101).

When de Man shifts from the thematic to the rhetorical register, the reality of Dionysos gets redefined: "He" becomes the effect rather than the cause of Apollonian appearance. Dionysos is an Apollonian dream that misrepresents itself as the representation of the unrepresentable Real and that misfigures itself as the metaphoric vehicle veiling a proper truth. The rhetorical reading performed not only by the critic but also by Nietzsche's text "puts into question the authority of metaphor as a paradigm of poetic language" (102). Here we stumble on de Man's problematic assertion, cited above, that under the pressure of this reading "metaphor becomes a blind metonymy, and the entire set of values that figure so prominently in *The Birth of Tragedy* . . . are made to appear hollow when they are exposed to the clarity of a new ironic light" (ibid.).[8] What—to ask it again—is a metonymy that can't "see"? Does "blind metonymy" refer metonymically to the blindness of the genetic or thematic reader who can't see the metonymy for the metaphor?

Some light on these questions may be thrown by de Man's next two chapters, which deal with the rhetoric of tropes and of persuasion, respectively, and which consider in more general terms the deconstructive practices at work in *The Birth of Tragedy*. De Man centers on the critique of the genetic fiction in which Nietzsche argues that logical priority "is uncritically deduced from a contingent temporal priority; we pair the polarities outside/inside and cause/effect on the basis of a temporal polarity before/after (or early/late) that remains unreflected." In this genetic or causal fiction the "outer, objective event in the world was supposed to determine the inner, conscious event as cause determines effect."

It turns out, however, that what was assumed to be the objective, external cause is itself the result of an internal effect. The result is "cumulative error, 'the consequence of all previous causal fictions,' which as far as the 'objective' world is concerned, are forever tied to 'the old error of original Cause.'"[9] In de Man's view, then, Nietzsche situates the genetic fiction in the rhetorical structure of discourse networks. It is "a linguistic event" (108) reified in the Aristotelian-type grammar and logic that reflect the operation of naive consciousness and that are enshrined in the tradition of Western Metaphysics.[10]

To deconstruct this operation is to expose the blind subjection of naive consciousness to the paralogism of inverse causality: If A is the cause of B, then B is the cause that A is a cause, and A's causality is therefore the effect of its effect. In de Man's words, "What had been considered to be a cause is, in fact, the effect of an effect, and what had been considered to be an effect can in its turn seem to function as the cause of its own cause."[11] Though "all rhetorical structures, whether we call them metaphor, metonymy, chiasmus, . . . or whatever, are based on substitutive reversals" of this sort (113), Nietzsche assigns the most fundamental "misinterpretation of reality," the reversal responsible for the genetic fallacy, to metonymy, which he defines as "the exchange or substitution of cause and effect," and which he considers to be "the paradigm of all language," one of his examples being, "revealingly enough, the substitution of 'tongue' for language."[12] This is the source of the blindness de Man attributes to metonymy—or, if his phrase "blind metonymy" is itself a metonymy, it is the source of the blindness the trope of genetic reversal produces in its users, who can't "see" it as reversal.

Since the result of de Man's reading of *Birth of Tragedy* is to establish the undecidability of the text, any attempt to identify, much less elaborate, a theory and a position attributable to Nietzsche may be misguided. Nevertheless, that's a risk worth taking because several passages from his posthumously published *Notebooks* articulate a coherent and consistent viewpoint that can stand as a contribution to an inquiry into metaphor and metonymy whether or not de Man, Nietzsche, or Nietzsche's text deconstructs it. Furthermore, although de Man makes much of Nietzsche's account of metonymy, he says very little about his occasionally odd treatment of metaphor, which I'll now review.

Nietzsche carries on his discussion of metaphor at two different levels, one very conventional and following—albeit critically—classical precedents, the other idiosyncratic and radical. In Lecture 3 of his posthumously published *Description of Ancient Rhetoric*—a lecture titled "The Relation of the Rhetorical to Language"—metaphor is briefly described as a trope that "does not produce new words, but gives new meaning to them," as in the foot or veins of a mountain and in the grammatical designation of gender, which he dismisses as "a luxury of language and pure metaphor."[13] In Lecture 7, after reviewing the names classical rhetoricians conferred on tropes, he glances at the definition, "the metaphor is a shortened simile," lists four different types of substitution, and then takes issue with Aristotle's different tetralogical scheme. He accepts as a proper type of transfer only Aristotle's category of figures constructed "according to proportion," which he illustrates by " 'as old age is to life, so evening is to day; thus, one can call evening the old age of day, or old age the evening of life' " (55–57). There are no surprises in this academic exercise.

There are surprises, however, in the introductory paragraphs of Lecture 3 and in passages scattered through the remainder of his unpublished writings. They are buried like mines in the former—buried (appropriately enough) in the rhetoric with which, after devoting two lectures to a review of ancient definitions and classifications of rhetoric, he unfolds his own revision of the pejorative modern attitude. But they break out in the editorial compilation titled "The Philosopher" and in the essay "On Truth and Lies in a Nonmoral Sense."[14]

In Lecture 3, which I consider first, Nietzsche lodges two complaints against his contemporaries: (1) "We" moderns use "rhetorical" as a term of "gentle reproof" that designates a forced and mannered departure from the "unrhetorical 'naturalness' of language," yet such naturalness is a myth, and we give it credence only because of (2) "our" failure to appreciate "that the true prose of antiquity is an echo of public speech [*der lauten Rede*] and is built upon its laws, whereas our prose is always to be explained more from writing, and our style gives itself as something to be perceived through reading."[15] He goes on to argue that "what is called 'rhetorical', as a means of conscious art, had been active as a means of unconscious art in language" from its origins. *Rhetoriké,* the formal art of rhetoric, is only "a further development . . . of the artistic means which are already found in language" (21). After briefly characterizing the three major tropes of synecdoche, metaphor, and metonymy, he concludes that "the tropes are not just occasionally added to words but constitute their most proper nature. . . . There is just as little distinction between actual words and tropes as there is between straightforward speech and rhetorical figures. What is usually called language is actually all figuration."[16]

But it isn't language alone that suffers tropical indirections. Nietzsche extends tropical power to the intertwined structures of linguistic and perceptual process, embedding rhetoricity in the human body's organic, psychological, and social interactions. He imagines these exchanges partly expedited and partly resisted by a conflicted dynamic that consists of both a set of overlapping forms of mediation and a set of disjunctions that prevent overlap. The "essence [Wesen] of language," he argues, is based no more than rhetoric on "the essence of things." Language has to do with persuasion, interpretation, and appropriation rather than with truth. Therefore its essence is "the power, which Aristotle calls rhetoric, . . . to discover and to impose whatever produces an effect and makes an impression,"[17] for language

> desires not to instruct, but to convey to others a subjective impulse and its acceptance. Man, who forms language [*Der sprachbildende Mensch*], perceives not things or events but impulses [*Reize*]: he communicates not sensations, but merely copies of sensations. The sensation, evoked through a nerve impulse [*einen Nervenreiz*], does not take in the thing itself: this sensation is presented externally through an image.[18]

With the first sentence—"[der Sprache] will nicht belehren, sondern eine subjektive Erregung und Annahme auf Andere übertragen"—Nietzsche plunges down to a murkier depth of analysis, one that fuses language, rhetoric, perception, and desire together as bodily functions of the sentient and desiring human agent. The translators' "impulse" tames "*Erregung*," which—like "*Reize*" below it—isn't confined here to its technical sense, "excitation," but glances beyond that toward stronger effects of arousal or excitement.[19] This in turn adds a charge that makes "Annahme" feel more like "submission" than like "acceptance": Whether as medium or as originary force, language is a desiring machine that produces effects of contagion, a machine that wishes to make its user—and to make its user wish to make others—experience and submit to whatever it expresses, whatever has attracted or charmed or irritated or teased this user.

The threat of contagion, however, is diminished by a rhetorical counterforce vested in the operation of the verb the translators render as "convey." This is the first occurrence in *Description* of a key Nietzschean term, "übertragen," "to carry over" (the literal translation), "to transfer" or "project" or "translate." Its root meaning, as Nietzsche's editors always point out, "is the same as the root meaning of the Greek verb *metapheró* (from which 'metaphor' is derived)."[20] Indeed, "in the sphere of rhetoric, *Übertragung* is the common German word for 'metaphor,' "[21] although later in the same text Nietzsche follows Quintilian and Cicero in claiming that it is what characterizes all tropes and distinguishes them from such rhetorical figures as the *schémata*, or figures of speech.[22]

Most important for our passage is the way Nietzsche maps the conflicted structure of metaphor onto the perceptual/linguistic process. The repeated "nicht . . . sondern" construction at once indicates and blocks the passage from the thing itself to the impulse to the sensation (*Empfindung*) to its reproduction (*Abbildung*) in "ein Bild," a (verbal) image, or "ein Tonbild," a sound-image (20–23). Thus every link in the mimetic chain conceptualized by correspondence theory (A is B is C is D) is broken (A is not B is not C is not D). A is B, but not really: The diachronic structure of perception-and-its-verbal-expression is analogous to that of metaphor. In this passage from Lecture 7 Nietzsche's focus is not on perception in general but on the perceptual and power relations involved in linguistic communication. By "power relations" I mean that the rhetorical context he sets up is implicitly—and ironically—Protagorean in the sense expressed by the following comment: Protagoras is "adept in rubbing his own appearances [things as they appear to his senses] into the minds of other people, instead of having theirs rub off on his."[23]

The subversive implications lurking in the passage just discussed surface in the aphoristic prose of "The Philosopher" and "On Truth and Lies in a Nonmoral Sense." There, more emphatically than in the passage from Lecture 3 of *Description* discussed above, Nietzsche massages metaphoricity into the perceptual process per se:

> Our sense perceptions are based, not upon unconscious inferences, but upon tropes. The primal procedure is to seek out some likeness between one thing and another, to identify like with like. Memory lives by means of this activity and practices it continually. . . . The senses of touch and vision provide [us with] two coexisting sensations and, since they always appear together, they arouse the idea of a connection (by means of a metaphor—for all things which appear together are not connected).[24]

> What power forces us to engage in imitation? The appropriation of an unfamiliar impression by means of metaphors. Stimulus and recollected image bound together by means of metaphor (analogical inference). Result: similarities are discovered and reanimated. A stimulus which has been repeated occurs once again in a recollected image.
>
> Stimulus perceived; now repeated in many metaphors, in the course of which related images from a variety of categories flock together. (50)
>
> The various languages placed side by side show that with words it is never a question of truth, . . . otherwise there would not be so many languages. The "thing in itself" . . . is likewise something quite incomprehensible to the [human being as] creator of language and something not in the least worth striving for. This creator only designates the relations of things to humans, and for expressing these relations he lays hold of the boldest metaphors. To begin with, a nerve stimulus is transferred onto an image [Ein Nervenreiz, zuerst übertragen in ein Bild]: first metaphor. The image, in turn, is imitated in a sound: second metaphor. And each time there is a complete overleaping of one sphere, right into the middle of an entirely new and different one. . . . It is this way with all of us concerning language: we believe that we know something about the things themselves when we speak of trees, colors, snow, and flowers: and yet we possess nothing but metaphors for things—metaphors which correspond in no way to the original entities. (82–83)

The tripartite structure of the percept as "first metaphor" has its termini in the object, the stimulus, and the image, each different from the other, so that the disenchanted judgment of experience may be expressed as a metaphoric copula: "The percept is [identical with] the object, but not really." Nevertheless, the mediating phase of the transfer from object to sensory stimulus often falls below the threshold of perception.[25] This gives rise to the mystified genetic intuition that the percept is an *imago rei,* a copy of its original. Nietzsche demystifies the intuition and locates it genealogically in the product of cultural consensus based on assent to a folk theory, the theory that the percept is an effect of the activity in which the passive sense organ receives the imprint of the object.

Nietzsche's characterization of perceptual process as metaphor obviously deprives that trope of its peculiar characteristic as a trope: the quality of conspicuous fictiveness inscribed in the formula, "A is B, but not really." Fictiveness remains, but it has become tacit rather than conspicuous. It has been displaced to the product of perception, whose metaphoricity, rooted in the element of negation, is concealed from that product. For this very reason fictiveness dominates perceptual process and embeds its human agents in a world of myth and irreality. Thus although what we take for real may actually be the fictional product of linguistico-perceptual elaboration, we say that the way it appears to us is the way it is. We act as if the percept is the effect and image of the object when in fact the linguistically mediated perceptual process—the way we perceive—is the cause of the object as we perceive it. It is only by becoming aware of the metaphoricity of this process that we can demystify the myth of perceptual mimesis.

Nietzsche's own comments on perception don't amount to the formal presentation of a theory of perception, but gestures toward such a theory appear throughout the notebooks of the early 1870s, and when these are collected, they coalesce into the following narrative: Between the image and its original falls the shadow of the stimulus (*der Nervenreiz*), which is not only a physiological effect but also a heteromorphic interpretation of the object. But if the stimulus is what the body registers, what it *re*ceives, it is not what we *per*ceive. The "recept" is not the percept. Nor is the percept an unmediated image delivered to and through the body.

Between the stimulus and the image fall the sound and sense of the word, and with them the whole cultural framework that includes concepts and categories. The percept is thus a linguistically coded and *heteromorphic* interpretation of the recept:

> Stimulus and recollected image bound together by means of metaphor (analogical inference). . . . Stimulus perceived; now repeated in many metaphors, in the course of which related images from a variety of categories flock together. . . . Knowing . . . wishes . . . to cling to the [sense] impression without metaphor. . . . But there is no "real" expression and no real knowing apart from metaphor. But deception on this point remains, i.e. the belief in a truth of sense impressions. The most accustomed metaphors, the usual ones, now pass for truths and as standards for measuring the rarer ones. . . . Knowing is nothing but working with the favorite metaphors. . . .[26]
>
> What then is truth? A movable host of metaphors, metonymies, and anthropomorphisms; in short, a sum of human relations that have been poetically and rhetorically intensified, transferred, and embellished. . . . Truths are illusions that we have forgotten are illusions.[27]

If we remembered—or ever knew—they were illusions, we would recognize them as metaphors. "Our primitive mode of contact with the world is essentially as artists, as more or less unwitting makers of images and metaphors, transforming rather than reproducing our experiences, themselves transformations rather than reproductions of their causes and objects."[28] In Nietzsche's theory, art is the model imitated by nature, and it is only on this deconstructive or genealogical basis that art can be said to imitate (itself as) nature.

Strangely enough, this theory of perception resembles in certain respects the one developed in Aristotle's *De Anima*. Aristotle structurally distinguishes the physiological process of *re*ception from the cognitive process of *per*ception by discussing the former in the second book of his treatise and the latter in the third. The division of books reflects and reinforces a distinction in theory between the recept, which includes the stimulus, and the percept. As St. Thomas Aquinas notes in his commentary on *De Anima,* the division reflects a substantive and not merely an organizational distinction. In Aquinas's revised but still faithful view of the *De Anima* theory, reception triggers perception, but whereas the vectors of reception go from world through body to mind, the vectors of perception go from mind through body to world. In a boustrophedon-like manner, perception turns around and folds over reception, and ends where it began.[29] This is a "realist" or mimetic theory in that it presupposes (and thus produces) correspondence between the "objective" cause of reception and its perceptual image.

Nietzsche's theory of perception is hardly realist. It is a theory about the epistemic power of language as rhetoric and of rhetoric as ideology. Its affiliations are with Humean skepticism and with such neo-Protagorean perspectivalists as Galileo. The realist theory is its target. But this critical genealogy notwithstanding, the perceptual process Nietzsche hypothesizes is structurally similar to Aristotle's in that he postulates a gap, a disconnection, between the recept and the percept. He also postulates a gap between the object and the recept, and adds a new element by insisting that the percept is sutured to a linguistico-phonetic unit. As in *The Birth of Tragedy,* there is both a naive genetic reading of the process and a deconstructive genealogical reading. The causal vector of the first is expressed by the formula object → recept → percept → word, that of the second by the formula word → percept → recept → object. The second mirrors or reverses the first, If we designate one formula as A and the other as B (it doesn't matter which is which), the relation between them assumes a familiar guise: A is B, but not really. The recept is the object, but not really. The percept is the recept, but not really.

In my introductory account of metaphor and metonymy I distinguish them as follows: Metaphor presents itself as an expressly false identity statement, an imaginary construction; metonymy presents itself as a transfer of the names of referents that are already coupled. Nietzsche's perspectivist approach both complicates and challenges this simple distinction. From the premise that perceptual data are always already interpretations influenced by language, he concludes that metaphor and metonymy work together to imprison us in a false reality:

> The drive toward the formation of metaphors is the fundamental human drive. . . . This drive is not truly vanquished and scarcely subdued by the fact that a regular and rigid new world is constructed as its prison from its own ephemeral products, the concepts. It seeks a new realm and another channel for its activity, and finds this in *myth* and *art* generally. This drive continually confuses the conceptual categories and cells by bringing forward new transferences, metaphors, and metonymies. It continually manifests an ardent desire to refashion the world which presents itself to waking man.[30]

Since metaphor doesn't declare itself as such in the work of perceptual tropes, only the deconstructive practices of art, poetry, philosophy, philology, and science can bring out the metaphoricity and thus the arbitrariness and creativeness of perception. But what about metonymy?

Metonymy is twice characterized in the lectures on rhetoric. In Lecture 3 it is curtly defined in a phrase that glances at the subversively paralogistic structure Nietzsche elsewhere calls "false inference": "the substitution of cause and effect [*Vertauschung von Ursache und Wirkung*]; for example, when the rhetor says 'perspiration' for 'work', 'tongue' for 'language.'"[31] In Lecture 7, "The Tropical Expression," he follows Quintilian in characterizing metonymy as "the placement of one noun for another, also called *hypallage* [an interchange, exchange], *cuius vis est, pro eo quod dicitur causam propter quam dicitur ponere* [the substitution of the cause for which we say a thing in place of the thing to which we refer]."[32] In "The Philosopher" and "On Truth and Lies in a Nonmoral Sense," Nietzsche occasionally lumps all the tropes together as variant forms of *Übertragung*, but for the most part he is pretty consistent, first, in distinguishing metaphor as a perceptually based trope from metonymy as a conceptually based trope, and second, in treating causal inversion as the identifying characteristic of metonymy.[33]

The most resonant account of the first distinction appears in "On Truth and Lies":

> Whereas each perceptual metaphor is individual and without equals and is therefore able to elude all classification, the great edifice of concepts displays the rigid regularity of a Roman columbarium and exhales in logic that strength and coolness which is characteristic of mathematics. Anyone who has felt this cool breath . . . will hardly believe that even the concept—which is as bony, foursquare, and transposable as a die—is nevertheless merely the residue of a metaphor.[34]

This "conceptual crap game," as Nietzsche calls it, derives its ironic force and carceral power from the second distinction, and the major virtue of de Man's analysis is to have emphasized and demonstrated the effect of Nietzsche's making metonymy the paradigmatic trope and the source of originary deception. When I slide his analysis under the account given above in my introductory discussion, that account gets modified as follows: In presenting itself as only a change of names that confirms the unified if complex order of reality, metonymy conceals both its preposterous structure and the transferential irreality it shares with metaphor, and thus imprisons us in a false world. What is really the case is that we have no access to what is really the case. A is B, but not really. Our metonymic relations with the world are fundamentally creative and metaphoric.[35]

Finally, it is worth pointing out that Nietzsche's deployment of Kantian concepts is loaded. First he conflates synthetic (a posteriori) judgments with paralogisms, or false inferences. Then he goes on to give the result his special stamp by mapping it on to his theory of tropes, identifying a particular mode of synthetic judgment—the paralogism of inverse causality—with the trope of metonymy.[36] Thus we read that "the only way to master manifoldness is by creating categories. . . . All explaining and knowing is actually nothing but categorization." The truth-status of categorization is wickedly exemplified by Thales's glide from the inductive generalization, "The entire world is moist," to the deductive principle, "Hence, the state of being moist is the essence of the entire world." Such "false inferences," Nietzsche claims, "are more accurately understood as metonymies, that is, rhetorically, poetically":[37]

> Abstractions are metonymies, that is, confusions of cause and effect. However, every concept is a metonymy, and knowledge occurs by means of concepts.[38]

> Every law of nature is ultimately a sum of anthropomorphic relations. . . .
>
> The essence of the definition: the pencil is an elongated, etc. body. A is B. In this instance what is elongated is also colored. The characteristics contain nothing but relations.
>
> A particular body is the equivalent of so many relations. Relations never can be the essence, but only the consequences of this essence. Synthetic judgment describes a thing according to its consequences, which means *essence* and *consequences are identified,* which means a *metonymy.*
>
> Thus a *metonymy* lies at the essence of synthetic judgment, which means it is a *false equation.*
>
> *Which means that synthetic inferences are illogical.* When we employ them, we presuppose popular metaphysics, that is, a metaphysics that regards effects as causes.

> The concept "pencil" is confused with the "thing" pencil. The "is" in the synthetic judgment is false, it contains a transference [*Übertragung*]; two distinct spheres, between which there never can be an equation, are placed next to each other.
>
> We live and think amid nothing but effects of the illogical, in lack of knowledge and incorrect knowledge.[39]

Why does Nietzsche here call an "Übertragung" that involves a false identity assertion or transference ("A is B") a metonymy rather than a metaphor? Because this particular transference involves not the superficially arbitrary yoking of two unlike things in different spheres of discourse but the conceptual reversal of cause and effect. Metonymy is more than a mere change of names; it is actually suppressed metaphor because it presupposes a fictive integration of experience into a unified set of orders, laws, and processes structured by the paralogism of inverse causality.[40]

FIVE

Metaphor, Metonymy, and Redundancy

My account of metaphor and metonymy in the preceding chapters suggests that if the difference between them is fluid, if it is weak in purely structural terms, it can be strengthened by contextualization. But a more serious problem confronts the effort to keep metaphor and metonymy apart. I've called them two fundamental tropes, or figures, and this means that I have already taken for granted a prior distinction: the distinction between the literal (or proper) and the figurative uses of language.

In this distinction, metonymy is a detour from literal usage that ultimately returns to it. Metonymy aspires only to emphasize or articulate the network of relations and substances of which the objects of literal reference are part. Metaphor is a more permanent detour, or no detour at all, but a diaspora, an exile that resists the return to the promised land of literalness. For this reason, metaphor was compelled for centuries to play second fiddle to metonymy.

Traditional language theory is imitative, or mimetic. It has, in Margaret Ferguson's words, "privileged proper over figurative language because the latter is seen as erring from the norms whereby each word points (univocally) to its referent. . . . But the very distinction between proper and figurative language is based on the notion of a source of significance which is fundamentally unaffected by the words which reflect it."[1] The source is paradoxically (or contradictorily) both inside and outside a system of which it is both center and origin. I illustrated this earlier in discussing the status of the empyrean as both the container of the cosmos, and the mind of God. In *Paradiso* 28, Dante expresses the paradox by an epiphany in which the order of spheres is turned inside out, with God at the center and the earth at the circumference.

This notion of source validates the organization of reality along the metonymic and analogical lines developed in Scholastic thought. We're familiar with the process by which the theory of language and reality discussed above has been destroyed. In W. V. O. Quine's bird's-eye view of it, "Things had essences, for Aristotle, but [for us) only linguistic forms have meanings. Meaning is what essence becomes when it is divorced from the object of reference and wedded to the word."[2] Today we find it easy to lend credence to the Nietzschean insight that classical, traditional, mimetic theories of language have been demystified, that ontology has been reduced to the study of language, and that our normal way of seeing the world, our natural attitude or standpoint, is a mere prejudice of Western Metaphysics. "A picture held us captive," Wittgenstein wrote, "and we could not get outside of it, for it lay in our language, and language seemed to repeat it to us inexorably."[3] But now that Western Metaphysics is on the skids, there is no obstacle to prevent us from seeing the truth, which is that the human mind and its language constitute reality.

The model for this constitutive act is the kind of pseudoreference we normally find, say, in prose fiction. A sentence like, "The man walked down the street," communicates to us, by its indicative style, the intention to denote an actuality, and it creates its referent in the act of denoting or indicating it. We know it is a fiction, but in the fictive ambience of the novel it has virtual reality. A paraphrase of Barthes's discussion of this phenomenon in *S/Z* puts it this way: "Denotation is shown to be a product, an effect, of connotation. . . . The final effect of connotation in the realist text is to produce the illusion of denotation, the illusion that language is incidental in the process of transcription of the real."[4]

Extended to language in general, this view posits figurality as the basic referential mode of language, a mode divisible into two orders, the figurative and the literal, with the literal being only a more devious or indirectly stated form of figurality. The distinction between metaphor and metonymy collapses with the collapse of the distinction between literal and figurative reference on which it's founded. Along with that, the privileged status of literal and metonymic reference vanishes. It is in this form that the problem of historical interpretation rises. To define metaphor and metonymy, even in the revised forms I give them here, is to activate a distinction that is conventional, the product of historical continuity and change. To destroy or deconstruct this conventional difference by reducing the two figures to a common structure is to take them out of history and to eliminate the possibility of articulating just those historical distinctions and interpretations that the difference between metaphor and metonymy enables.

The effect of this move is to make language and perception together conspire to deceive us about their true nature. They are creative and yet they present themselves as imitative. They are figural and yet they present themselves as literal. Carried to an extreme, this disenchanted insight can lead to elitist, structuralist, and antihistorical conclusions—the conclusion, for example, that most of history and humankind have been, and are, in the state of bad faith or false consciousness. What could be more seriously afflicted with this disease than the pathetically naive Middle Ages? Their whole universe was a fiction, a cosmic tinkertoy, invented and modified by humans, yet they had the stupidity and effrontery to ascribe it to God, and the greater stupidity and effrontery to create a God to ascribe it to.

But we don't have to carry the insight to this extreme. In fact, we can head it in the opposite direction by using it to help us establish a more sympathetic rapport with earlier and other cultures. The insight is startling, difficult, and unsettling, not because it did away with poor old Western Metaphysics, but because it goes against the grain of our perceptual and linguistic habits. It violates naive consciousness. Yet to say that is to remind you that naive consciousness is alive and well. It still repeats to us inexorably the picture that held us captive, and though Wittgenstein can interpret naive consciousness, he can't change it.

What this suggests is that language and perception are the products of the logic of evolution. Their imitative or realistic prejudices must have evolved over the eons into ecologically functional adaptations. Among the most important of these prejudices is the process by which perception and language misrepresent themselves in pretending that the world they create is a world they passively receive and accurately reflect. I don't think it stretches usage to call this basic process something like demetaphorizing, or literalizing.

Metonymizing is also a process, connected to literalizing. It may be illustrated by the extension or transfer of terms of consanguinity to nonlineal structures of kinship and authority; by the transfer of the concept of "blood" to a part of generative process and structure; by the transfer of terms signifying consciousness and personality to natural phenomena; by the transfer of personal names to tribes and areas; and by the transfer of terms for social order to cosmic order (and vice versa). In pointing out the fictive or constitutive nature of such metonymizing activity, the modern critic indicates a double process at the root of perception, language, and thought.

In this process, (1) the mind appears freely to improvise metaphoric connections between different items and orders of experience, and (2) it conceals this from naive consciousness by demetaphorizing, or metonymizing, these connections. The mind's improvisations may appear freer than they are, for perception has evolved in terms of certain adaptive constraints and probabilities, and it reveals the marks of these conditions in a set of coherently related preferences or prejudices. The most important prejudice of perception is its tendency to transcendentalize experience by presenting it as given and received to a much greater degree than is actually the case.

This is what it means to say that the extent to which the mind operates on the world is concealed by the extent to which the world seems to operate on the mind. Such a hidden dialectic could only be brought out into the open by the counterperceptual critique of Western Metaphysics—a critique that has been going on for many centuries and that in one of its more recent forms has been assigned the name *deconstruction*. The effect of this critique is to remetaphorize the basic relation of language to reality. But if this makes us see that literalizing, or demetaphorizing, has deceived us about the nature of language, it also leads to the inference that the deception must have met some adaptive need and served some ecological purpose.

It isn't hard to guess what that purpose is. Existentialism offers one explanation: the human need to trade the anxiety of freedom for the security of determinism. But I prefer to describe the adaptive purpose in the language of cybernetics, which, as we'll see, has closer formal affiliations to linguistic phenomena, and especially to the rhetorical process of metonymizing. The particular cybernetic concept I have in mind is that of redundancy.

The concept of redundancy in information science has been variously interpreted, and I give two versions, the first more negative than the second. "What," asks Max Black, "is achieved by receiving a correct message?" and he identifies one possible answer: "reduction of uncertainty." When the interrogator asks a yes-or-no question, uncertainty is removed by the answer.

The communications engineer seeks to make this procedure as accurate and efficient as possible, but he and the communicators face an obstacle that complicates the situation: The "enemy is noise, here used in the technical sense of unintended and unpredictable extra signals." Noise, which "can be reduced, counteracted, but never altogether eliminated," introduces an additional source of uncertainty. One way to counteract this uncertainty

> is to increase the redundancy of the message. A message is said to be "redundant" when it includes more symbols than are needed to carry its information: if the message sent . . . were "Yes yes" it would be more redundant than a plain yes. . . . Redundancy reduces the efficiency of the message, but is a prophylactic against misinterpretation.[5]

Redundancy does not affect the meaning of the message. It is a change of pattern, a repetition for emphasis which is intended to ensure that the meaning will be accurately received. Redundancy as a kind of amplifying device aims to increase comprehension and reduce the probability of wrong guessing. It may enhance expressive force and have affective value as an instrument of persuasion. But it is chiefly the reduction of uncertainty to which I now want to draw attention.

Black's account of redundancy is formalistic. He takes for granted the necessary semantic precondition of redundancy—that there be a code, a whole, a *Gestalt,* a *langue* which gives meaning to the parts of messages. And while his emphasis on the reduced efficiency of redundant coding is applicable to communications theory, other contexts in which part-whole relations are stressed reveal its efficiency, in the sense of economy.

Associative learning is one such context. For example, Ralph Berger asks what adaptive value could be served by "afferent-afferent associations, or what is known as sensory-sensory learning," for example, "the emergence of the visual image of a flower in response to its scent." His answer is

> that the innate nervous system has an economically finite number of connections, and this requires the development of a certain redundancy in perception and experience. If afferent activity in an innate feature-detecting system of neurons, denoting one feature of a stimulus, is repeatedly accompanied by afferent activity denoting another sensory feature not in an innate feature-detecting system, the learned association of the two would allow an animal to detect the stimulus and register its adaptive significance even when the genetically selected feature was absent. Information theory has shown the functional significance of redundancy. In spelling, for example, considerable redundancy exists such that several characters can be absent without loss of comprehension. The natural selection of only one or two primary features of an event for genetically predetermined detection by the brain is highly economic if a process is also provided for the learning of other features of the object by association. This economy therefore constitutes the adaptive value of afferent-efferent learning.[6]

The image and scent of a flower are redundant in a sense very different from the "Yes Yes" of Black's example. Afferent-afferent associations are redundant in that any of a number of different percepts could serve to identify the same object. Their relation to the object is precisely that of metonymy; they are parts standing for wholes. Since the act of metonymic association presupposes some code in which wholes and parts are already analyzed, it might be more useful to think of redundancy as an ordering principle that makes such substitutions and representations possible.

This freer interpretation of the concept has been put into play by Gregory Bateson:

"Meaning" may be regarded as an approximate synonym of pattern, redundancy, information, and "restraint," within a paradigm of the following sort:

Any aggregate of events or objects (e.g., a sequence of phonemes, a painting, or a frog, or a culture) shall be said to contain "redundancy" or "pattern" if the aggregate can be divided in any way by a "slash mark," such that an observer perceiving only what is on one side of the slash mark can guess, with better than random success, what is on the other side of the slash mark. We may say that what is on one side of the slash contains information or has meaning about what is on the other side. Or, in engineer's language, the aggregate contains "redundancy." . . . Examples:

The letter T in a given location in a piece of written English prose proposes that the next letter is likely to be an H or an R or a vowel. It is possible to make a better than random guess across a slash which immediately follows the T. English spelling contains redundancy.

From a part of an English sentence, delimited by a slash, it is possible to guess at the syntactic structure of the remainder of the sentence.

From a tree visible above ground, it is possible to guess at the existence of roots below ground. The top provides information about the bottom.[7]

Thus Bateson defines redundancy as the "patterning or predictability of particular events within a larger aggregate of events" (406):

If I say to you "It is raining," this message introduces redundancy into the universe, message-plus-raindrops, so that from the message alone you could have guessed—with better than random success—something of what you would see if you looked out of the window. (408)[8]

> If now we turn away from the narrow universe of message structure and consider the outer world of natural phenomena, we observe at once that this outer world is similarly characterized by redundancy, i.e., that when an observer perceives only certain parts of a sequence or configuration of phenomena, he is in many cases able to guess . . . at the parts which he cannot immediately perceive. It is, indeed, a principal goal of the scientist to elucidate these redundancies or patternings of the phenomenal world. (414)
>
> It will be noted that this way of thinking about communication groups all methods of coding under the single rubric of part-for-whole. (415)

The orders generated by such methods are patterns that reduce uncertainty by creating redundancy and making predictability possible. To see something as a part and to be able to predict what lies unseen beyond the slash presupposes not only knowledge of but also belief in a prior whole. The principle of redundancy is monocosmic. Whole and part, macrocosm and microcosm, are posited or constituted in the same process of transposition.

A major "goal" of the process is to organize wholes that traditional "scientists"—seers, shamans, priests, elders—can elucidate. Thus, given a certain organization of cosmos and kinship, "from a tree visible above ground" it may be possible to guess at the existence of a divine person or ancestor below ground, and to perform the appropriate act of approach or avoidance. A particular system of classificatory kinship enables subjects to make a better than random guess at the different samples of behavior expected from and by different mothers or fathers or brothers. The system determines the boundaries of the behavioral repertory as a whole. It distributes its "part-behaviors" among the different kinship roles. In such ways, redundancy provides the incomplete directions that evoke and orient the exercise of art.

I stated earlier that metonymy is only superficially a mere change of names. It is actually suppressed metaphor because it presupposes a fictive integration of experience into a unified set of orders, laws, and processes. The totalizing formula of the metaphoric "A is B" may be expressed in a variety of ways, for example, "experience is a unified whole," "the world is a spherical cosmos," "the social order reflects the cosmic order," "the psychic order reflects the social order," "God created humanity in His image," "positive (human) law is derived from natural law." In every case, the outside observer discerns a contradictory ("A is not B") that the formula dogmatically suppresses.

In some cases the contradictory takes the form of an inversion: The cosmic order may be an image derived from the social order. Human beings created nature and natural law as well as the forms of divinity to which they ascribe those creations. The examples just given are examples of what Willard Van Orman Quine calls "cultural posits."[9] Suppressing the contradictory, converting metaphor to metonymy, changes a posit to a deposit. By treating terms as if they were merely names, metonymy displaces (de-posits) modifications of meaning from language to reality.

The metonymizing process I've been describing serves two functions:

1. It activates the principle of redundancy to integrate experience into a cosmos. Through the operation of redundancy experience is simplified, ordered, and enriched, and the values of the cultural attitude are expressively inscribed in the multiplicity of structures and practices. Two examples focused on the symbolism of the house will suggest how this works.

Marshall Sahlins has shown in detail how the construction of the Moalan house "is in material form and division of labor a tangible representation" of the structure of relationships informing Moalan kinship, production, and polity, and how each of these codes functions as a "medium by which a system of culture is realized as an order of action":

> The isomorphism between architectural and general cultural categories is . . . something more than a picturesque analogy. Insofar as the house is . . . divided symbolically, it becomes the construction of a comparable differentiation of behavior. . . . What is in analysis a set of parallel classifications, or a single structure operating on different planes, is in experience an undivided totality. . . . Unfolding in a habitation so structured, the relationships between persons are themselves inhabited by the same structure.[10]

There is a double redundancy at work here: one structure inscribed in many different spheres and objects; one sphere or object invested with many different meanings. This complementarity distributes the whole in all its parts and assimilates the parts to each other in ways that reinforce the dominance of attitude over structure.

From an analysis of the Kabyle house, Pierre Bourdieu draws a similar conclusion in a passage that anticipates the second of the two functions of metonymy:

> Through the magic of a world of objects which is the product of the application of the same schemes to the most diverse domains, a world in which each thing speaks metaphorically [i.e., metonymically] of all the others, each practice comes to be invested with an objective meaning, a meaning with which practices—and particularly rites—have to reckon at all times, whether to evoke or revoke it. . . . All the symbolic manipulations of body experience, starting with displacements within a mythically structured space, e.g., the movements of going in and coming out, tend to impose the integration of the body space with cosmic space by grasping in terms of the same concepts (and naturally at the price of great laxity in logic) the relationship between man and the natural world and the

complementarity and opposed states and actions of the two sexes in the division of sexual work and sexual division of work, and hence in the work of biological and social reproduction.[11]

2. The second adaptive function of the metonymizing process is to invest the products of redundancy "with an objective meaning." So long as human beings are vitally affected by forces they recognize as—or forces they are persuaded are—beyond human control, they are compelled to find ways to deal with those forces, to make contact with them, to exert influence over them. One way both to increase predictability and to diminish apprehensiveness is to transpose personlike presences into the world so that transcendent reality may appear conscious of the existence and needs of human beings. When ideological labor brings forth a divine Cause as its effect, it lays the groundwork for a whole set of subsidiary causal agents made "in its image"—fathers, kings popes, priests, and emperors. Metonymy naturalizes, and redundancy enforces, the authority of each agent.

Suppose, to repeat Gregory Bateson's example, I see the top part of a tree and view it as part of a divine person in the ground. Then I have either metaphorized or metonymized, depending on whether culture disapproves or approves of this interpretation. Metonymizing, which is subject to cultural approval, is a way of making real, making transcendent. The function or effect of metaphor is to diminish redundancy and to offer fictive alternatives to culturally approved reality. The value of metaphor is not something that would be readily appreciated in an age that depends on metonymizing for its most important practical and spiritual orientations. Metonymy is traditional where metaphor is modern, conservative where metaphor is radical or subversive.

SIX

The Semiotics of Metaphor and Metonymy: Umberto Eco

Nietzsche is fundamentally concerned with the circuitous and deceptive character of our relations to things, and with the transcendence of actuality to our representations of it at the level of the signifier. But to a semiotician, the distinction between linguistic activity and extralinguistic reality is naive, and so I turn to Umberto Eco's more doggedly semiotic approach to this distinction in *A Theory of Semiotics*. Eco divides semiotics into two parts: the theory of codes or signification and the theory of sign-production or language use. *Code* designates the system of rules that "generate signs as concrete occurrences in communicative intercourse."[1] He devotes the first part to the analysis of relations between signifier and signified and the second part to the analysis of sign/referent relations.

Eco is uncomfortable with traditional accounts of reference that ignore the semiotic conditions which make acts of mentioning or referring possible. He insists that we can't mention or refer to objects unless they have already been constituted as such by the coding process that produces the semiotic entities to which the objects correspond. Even the organization and segmentation of the perceptual field is linguistically coded and therefore presupposes cultural coding.

His vocabulary is carefully chosen to accommodate a disciplined reduction of the world of referents to a continuously active and changing "semantic global universe."[2] He replaces the conventional term "sign" by the term "sign-function" in order to emphasize the dynamic, transitory, and provisional character of any semiotic correlation. "Signifier" gives way to "sign-vehicle" and "verbal expression" (and occasionally "lexeme"), while "content" or "seme" and "sememe" replace "signified."[3] The concept of referent is conspicuously excluded from this system—or at least it is accessible only if its semiotic representation has already been established.[4]

Eco's resistance to traditional reference theory is primarily methodological. His aim is to shift the consideration of the pragmatics of reference from the analysis of the theory of codes to the analysis of the theory of sign production. But this resistance also has a target in view: the position of philosophers who maintain "that a sign is only a sign when it is used in order to name things" and who try "to demonstrate that a notion of meaning as separated from the 'real' and verifiable 'denotatum' of the sign, that is, the object or the state of the world to which the sign refers, is devoid of any real purport."[5] Against this argument he insists that

> the semiotic object of a semantics is the *content*, not the referent, and the content has to be defined as a *cultural unit* (or as a cluster or a system of interconnected cultural units). . . . The referential fallacy consists in assuming that the "meaning" of a sign-vehicle has something to do with its corresponding object. (62)

> Take the term /dog/. The referent will certainly not be the dog *x* standing by me while I am pronouncing the word. For anyone who holds to the doctrine of the referent, the referent, in such a case,

> will be all existing dogs (and also all past and future dogs). But «all existing dogs» is not an object which can be perceived with the senses. It is a set, a class, a logical entity.
>
> *Every attempt to establish what the referent of a sign is forces us to define the referent in terms of an abstract entity which moreover is only a cultural convention.* (66)

On this basis Eco insists that acts of referring and their objects in extralinguistic reality have no place in a theory of codes. The empirical subjects who refer and the objects they refer to cannot per se be admitted into "Global Semantic Space."[6] Semiotics does not deny their existence or influence. Rather, it transforms them by reducing them to semiotic functions the interactivity of which is represented within the theory of sign production.

Eco's long chapter on sign production is organized in terms of the different types of labor required "to produce and interpret signs, messages or texts" (152). Under the category of rhetorical labor, he discusses metaphor and metonymy as "typical rhetorical figures" (280). After nodding toward Roman Jakobson's similarity-versus-contiguity thesis, he quietly proceeds to displace Jakobson's distinction from things to elements and relations within the dynamic field of a "semantic universe" that undergoes "unlimited semiosis."[7]

His first example is an analogy between Dominican friars and dogs that *could* be based on their attributes as entities in the world, but that Eco prefers to base on the echoic similarity between their signifiers:

> Granted that both the sememe « dog » and the sememe « friar » possess the same connotative marker of « fidelity » (to their master) and « defense » (dogs defend their masters and friars defend the principles of religion) it was easy during the twelfth century to invent for an order of mendicant friars (the Dominicans) the metaphor "dogs of God" (*domini canes*). In this way the notion of 'similarity' no longer involves a suspected resemblance based on the

> thing itself . . . ; a 'similarity' between semantic markers is simply a *semic identity*. On the other hand metonymy often seems to be a simple matter of overcoding; substitution by syntagmatic contiguity is based on the fact that, given a ready-made syntagm, established habits will permit one of its elements to be substituted for another. Thus given the accepted semiotic judgment /the President of the United States officially lives in the White House/ it is easy to use /the White House/ as a metonymy for /the President of the United States/.[8]

"Friars are dogs, but not really": the metaphoric analogy is motivated by the function of defense dogs and friars share. Nevertheless, Eco's uncoupling of meaning from reference deprives the analogy of the operation that metaphor presupposes. The portability or transferability of meaning from "dogs of God" to "an order of mendicant friars" is etymologically preestablished—"simply a *semic identity*." His dismissive use of "simply" makes it clear that Eco's interest is in the meaning-effect arbitrarily produced by the purely formal resemblance between the two expressions or sign vehicles, *Dominicanes* and *domini canes*.

This resemblance is available without the help of the connotative links of « fidelity » and « defense. » Yet when Eco goes on to say of his presidential example that the metonymy is a case not of "semic identity" but of "semic interdependence," the weight of his contrast falls on "the fact" that "living in the White House is conventionally accepted as a semantic property of the cultural unit 'President of the U.S.'" This emphasizes the preexistence of the metonymized relationship to its linguistic expression. Preexistence is a more basic feature of metonymy than spatial contiguity or containment, which are special cases of it.

As Eco himself points out (310), his "Dominicans / domini canes" is almost too perfect an example of metaphor. It is generated from the arbitrary and accidental overlap of sign-vehicles that produces a pun. What he calls "semic identity," however, is the identity not of the signifiers but of the connotative markers "fidelity" and "defense." A glance first at two of his provisional distinctions between denotative and connotative markers, and then at one of his semiotic perspectives on the copula, will disclose an important criterion that underlies Eco's distinction between metaphor and metonymy.

Denotative markers are "those whose sum (or hierarchy) constitutes and isolates the cultural unit which first corresponds to the sign-vehicle." What the sign-vehicle *de*notes is "a network of positions within the same semantic system." For "dog," the system might be the zoological code, but not the ecclesiastico-religious code. What the sign-vehicle *con*notes is "a network of positions within different semantic systems." Connotative markers "contribute to the constitution of one or more other cultural units expressed by the preceding sign-function" (85–86).

The difference between denotative and connotative markers is that the second presupposes and relies on the first. In denotation "the code makes a sign-vehicle correspond" to "one of the positions within a semantic system . . . without any previous mediation," but a connotative correspondence can arise only "through the mediation of a previous denotative marker" (85). On this basis, Eco formulates a second provisional pair of definitions that are applicable to a theory of sign production and that take account of the factor of reference:

> (a) a denotation is a cultural unit or semantic property of a given sememe which is at the same time a culturally recognized property of its possible referents;
>
> (b) a connotation is a cultural unit or semantic property of a given sememe conveyed by its denotation and not necessarily corresponding to a culturally recognized property of the possible referent.[9]

How do these definitions bear on our distinction between metaphor and metonymy? Let's consider the following examples:

1. "rose" stands for "love"
   "dogs of God" stands for "friars"
2. "sail" stands for "ship"
   "White House" stands for "President"

We can rewrite "stands for" as the copula "is" without too much strain by adopting Eco's definition of "is" as "a metalinguistic sign that means 'possesses some of the semantic properties of.'"[10] Then the difference between the two sets may be expressed as follows. "Rose" has no intrinsic relation to "love," nor does "dogs" to "friars." But a sail is part of a ship, and the White House is the President's home. In each example in the first set one sememe possesses some of the semes of the other with respect to connotative markers but not to denotative markers. In the second set the sememe pairs are denotatively as well as connotatively related.[11]

In these examples, the important distinction between metaphor and metonymy lies in their different relations to "culturally recognized" properties of the paired sememes that are specified by the presence or absence of denotative relations which signify "semic" interdependence. On the one hand, semic identity in metaphors is asserted in the absence of semic interdependence. On the other hand, in each metonymic pair both terms are denotatively related. Both thus occupy positions within the same semantic system as members (part for whole, concrete for abstract, container for contained) of a cultural unit that is a "ready-made syntagm."

At this juncture the semiotic explanation converges on the educated lay view I unpacked earlier. "Metonymy" names all tropes in which the transfer of semantic properties is mediated and motivated by relationships that preexist their linguistic appearance in figurative expressions. "Metaphor" names all tropes in which connotative transfer is unmediated and unmotivated by prior denotative relationships, and indeed in which such relationships are conspicuously disregarded, so that the transfer appears to be constituted within and by its linguistic expression.

The semiotic and lay explanations thus seem to agree, and we return to the formula stated above: The central difference between metaphor and metonymy derives from their contrary relations to actuality. Yet this agreement may be short-lived when viewed from the semiotic standpoint since, as I noted, my reason for introducing that standpoint is to question the naive distinction between linguistic activity and extralinguistic reality. And although the semiotic revision of the distinction exemplified in Eco's theory is satisfactory as far as it goes, we'll see that it doesn't go far enough and that it leads to another question.

For lay approaches to semantics it is enough to analyze the field of inquiry into two subfields, that of the system of signs and that of the system of referents, and to valorize them according to such models as the infamous nature/culture distinction. In traditional theory, reality is prior to language, is different from but reflected by language, and is unaffected by language. The structuralist critique initiated by Saussure bracketed out the domain of reference implicated in language use. It did this by dissociating the semiotic system from semiotic process and concentrating on the internal signifier/signified relationships of the sign.

Roughly contemporaneous with Saussure was the initiation of the study of reference in another field of inquiry, that of the language philosophers (Frege, Russell, Wittgenstein, Strawson, Quine, Kripke, et al.), and the resultant split for a long time left relations between the study of the sign and the study of reference in confusion. This confusion was not helped by the fact that Saussure considered the domain of language use too "heterogeneous" to be reducible to systematic analysis. In effect, he consigned speech to "reality." One of Eco's important moves was to go back to a philosopher whose work predated the split and subsumed both fields under a broader conception of unified general semiology: Charles Sanders Peirce. Eco's theory explicitly unfolds as a continuous revision of Peirce's "pragmaticism," a revision dedicated to "de-mentalizing" Peircean concepts.

Although Eco, like Saussure, dissociates the semiotic system from semiotic process, he differs in treating both system and process as dialectically interrelated objects of theoretical analysis. The system is analyzed by the theory of codes, and the process by the theory of sign production. He insists that this is a methodological rather than an ontological reduction. Nevertheless, it has nontrivial implications for an ontology that includes (as Eco's does) empirical subjects and objects of reference. For whether these subjects and objects become significant, whether they negotiate the crossing from factual to semiotic existence, depends on their ability to accommodate themselves to the prevailing codes and modes of sign production. According to Eco, semiotic representations do not depend on the existence of the things they represent:

> Semiotics is concerned with everything that can be taken as a sign. A sign is everything which can be taken as significantly substituting for something else. This something else does not necessarily have to exist or . . . actually be somewhere at the moment in which the sign stands for it. Thus semiotics is in principle the discipline studying everything which can be used in order to lie. (7)

Semiotics may thus properly claim to be the study of the production of ideology, given a certain understanding of ideology.

Eco produces this reduction by analytically separating an object from its "content." For example, of such indicators as demonstratives he claims that they have "first of all a content, a marker of « proximity » or « closeness » independently of the actual closeness of an object" (164). Even more radically, and in a Nietzschean spirit, he maintains that the segmentation of the perceptual field into objects presupposes cultural coding: "The attribution of a cultural unit to the field of perceptual stimuli" (167) produces the content or sign-function that underlies any act of referring.

Percepts can be treated as signs because something more than meets the eye always meets the eye. "In order to assert that objects (insofar as they are perceived) can also be approached as signs, one must also assert that even the concepts of objects (as the result or as the determining schema of every perception) must be considered in a semiotic way" (166). From this it follows that

> even when the referent could be the object named or designated by the expression when language is used in order to mention something, one must nonetheless maintain that an expression does not, in principle, designate any object, but on the contrary conveys a cultural content. . . . The semiotic object of a semantics is the *content,* not the referent, and the content has to be defined as a *cultural unit.* . . . (61–62)

> We may commonly speak of a thing called Alpha Centauri, but we have never experienced it. An astronomer has occasionally experienced it with some strange apparatus. But we do not know this astronomer. We only know a cultural unit communicated to us by means of words, drawings, or other means. (66)

> Now, there was a time when all (or most) of the employees [working in offices] wore white collars on their shirts. This contiguity was codified, and only at that moment was it possible to designate the employees as "white-collar workers"; even if today there are no employees wearing white collars, one can recognize that this contiguity is capable of founding a metonymic substitution. This is a sign that the contiguity is no longer factual but semiotic. What matters is, not that in reality someone wears white collars, but that

in a semantic representation of the lexeme /employee/ there exists the connotation « wears white collars ».[12]

The point of this semiotic bracketing is not that language as an abstracted system has no relation to reality because it consists only of items that are positioned, posited—or indeed, not posited but deposited—in the graveyard and womb of reference whose plots Eco calls cultural units. Rather, the point is that the ghosts of Reference Past are packed into each sememe, and into the system as a whole, as in an encyclopedia.[13] There, seemingly inert between acts of reference, they flourish underground in networks of denotation and connotation that crisscross in the profusion of "unlimited semiosis":

> Culture continuously translates signs into other signs, and definitions into other definitions, words into icons, icons into ostensive signs, ostensive signs into new definitions, new definitions into propositional functions, propositional functions into exemplifying sentences and so on; in this way it proposes to its members an uninterrupted chain of cultural units composing other cultural units, and thus translating and explaining them. (71)

Eco's revised approach to the relation of language to "reality" generates two outcomes. The first is that the scope of reference is constrained by the organization of semiotic codes. This organization at any given moment influences even the segmentation of the perceptual field, since objects along with their contents—and the relations between them—are cultural units produced by semiosis. Eco puts this in a more positive way: "An act of mentioning or referring is made possible by a very complicated previous semiosic process which has already constituted the perceived object as a semiotic entity" (167). His view of the domination of reference by code is apparent in a passage in which he changes the values implicit in the Fregean scheme of *Zeichen* (sign) / *Sinn* (sense or meaning) / *Bedeutung* (reference):

> To say that /Walter Scott/ and /the author of Waverly/ are two expressions that have the same *Bedeutung* but two *Sinn* concerns a theory of sign-function only insofar as: (i) the *Bedeutung* is intended as the definition of a historical entity that a culture recognizes as a single person, and is therefore a denoted content; (ii) the *Sinn* is a particular way of considering a given content, according to other cultural conventions, thereby including within one's consideration some of the connoted contents of the first denoted content.
>
> If one assumes that the *Bedeutung* is an actual state of the world, whose verification validates the sign, one must ask oneself how this state of the world is usually grasped or analyzed. . . . It will quickly be seen that, in order to know something about the *Bedeutung*, one must indicate it through another expression, and so on; as Peirce said, a sign can be explained only through another sign. Thus the *Bedeutung* is grasped through a series of its *Sinn*, and in this sense . . . it is the *Bedeutung* which is defined by the *Sinn* and not vice versa. (61)

The second outcome of Eco's revision is that since the process of unlimited semiosis is accessible to diachronic as well as synchronic analysis, semiotics can consider the contribution of reference and sign production to the continuous changing of the code:

> In exchanging messages and texts, judgments and mentions, people contribute to the changing of codes. This social labor can be either openly or surreptitiously performed; thus a theory of code-changing must take into account the public reformulation of sign-functions and the surreptitious code-switching performed by various rhetorical and ideological discourses. (152)

This dialectic between codes and messages, whereby codes control the emission of messages, but new messages can restructure the codes, constitutes the basis for a discussion on the creativity of language and on its double aspect of "rule-governed creativity" and "rule-changing creativity." (161)

In order to make semiotic theory sensitive to this dialectic, Eco rejects Saussure's notion of a sign as "a fixed semiotic entity" and replaces it with the concept of sign-functions as "the provisional result of coding rules which establish transitory correlations" between expression (lexeme) and content (sememe). Since "each of these elements . . . [is] entitled to enter—under given coded circumstances—into another correlation and thus form a new sign . . . the classical notion of 'sign' dissolves itself into a highly complex network of changing relationships" (49). Eco pictures the transformed field as "a sort of molecular landscape in which what we are accustomed to recognize as everyday forms turn out to be the result of transitory chemical aggregations and so-called 'things' are only the surface appearance assumed by an underlying network of more elementary units" (ibid.).

At this point, we encounter a problem in Eco's theoretical approach. Given two variables, (1) the semantico-cultural system and its codes, and (2) particular acts of sign production or reference, conventional practice holds (1) steady in order to explore distinctions in (2). Furthermore, to a greater or lesser degree conventional practice identifies the system and its codes with "actuality" or "extralinguistic reality," and this sometimes has the effect of reifying as "natural" what Eco treats as the system's methodologically motivated stability.

Eco's theory is in principle designed to block or demystify these conventional moves. Yet in practice, his eagerness to stress the influence of meaning on reference leads him to hold the field of cultural units steady.[14] He brackets its variability because he is primarily concerned with the way in which acts of mentioning or referring mobilize the resources of the *existing* linguistic code. He is less interested in the way "new messages . . . semantically restructure the code,"[15] a topic he assigns to the study of ideology. "For a semiotics of codes there is no need to establish how the message comes into existence nor for what political or economic reasons; instead, it is concerned to establish in what sense this new coding can be called 'ideological'" (290).

One result of this restriction crops up in Eco's treatment of metaphor and metonymy. In "The Semantics of Metaphor" he shows how any metaphor "can be traced back to a subjacent chain of metonymic connections that constitute the framework of the code and upon which is based the constitution of any semantic field, whether partial or (in theory) global." In a model based on unlimited semiosis, "every sign, sooner or later, must depend upon a connection anticipated by the code."[16]

When these connections are visualized as a network of pathways, we can see why metonymy gets defined in terms of contiguity and why Eco characterizes language as "a multidimensional network of metonymies, each of which is explained by a cultural convention rather than by an original resemblance" (78). Not merely "factual (empirical) contiguity" but "contiguity of code" instituted by cultural design makes it possible for "crown" to stand for "king" and "sail" for "ship" (79–80). One term can connote the other because their denotations are semantically interdependent: "Metonymic chains [are] based . . . on identifiable semantic structures" (69).

Eco explains metaphor in terms of this explanation of metonymy. Metaphoric substitutions are "short circuits of a preestablished path," and they can only take place "because of the existence in the code of connections and therefore contiguities" and therefore metonymies (81, 79). A metaphor, he claims, is more or less rewarding as "its metonymic foundation" is less or more evident (82)—as the pathway that joins the underlying metonyms is more or less circuitous.

Because "inventive" metaphors draw unlikely or previously unthought-of connections "from the interior of the circle of unlimited semiosis . . . they cannot easily be accepted; the system tends not to absorb them." They produce "'information' in the most proper sense of the term: an excess of disorder in respect to existing codes"

(86–87). Eco outlines the process by which metaphoric couplings that are "still not a part of our culture" become domesticated. Either they become customary and enter the code as metonymies ("the mouth of the bottle," "the leg of the table") or else, as anticipations of new knowledge, they contribute to a restructuring of the code. In both cases metaphor, which was initially strange, subversive, or countercultural, has "turned into culture" (79, 87) and has assumed the ontologically modest character of metonymy. By pretending to indicate only relations that exist before they enter linguistic form, metonymy covers over the fundamental creativity and figurality of language. Thus if metaphor is collapsed metonymy, metonymy is suppressed metaphor. Just such a suppression converts ideology into reality. But this isn't a unidirectional process: If metaphoric transfers may become metonymic, metonymic transfers may turn back into metaphors. The next chapter briefly considers a text that glances at the dilemma of figural reversibility and hints at its pathos.

SEVEN

Frost and Roses: The Disenchantment of a Reluctant Modernist

The text is a short poem by Robert Frost entitled "The Rose Family":

> The rose is a rose,
> And was always a rose.
> But the theory now goes
> That the apple's a rose,
> And the pear is, and so's
> The plum, I suppose.
> The dear only knows
> What will next prove a rose.
> You, of course, are a rose—
> But were always a rose.

This is an adventure in conspicuous redundancy: ten lines with a single rhyme and with the same end word in six of those lines. The first line alludes to and varies Gertrude Stein's mischievous tautology, substituting "The rose" for the indefinite "A rose" that Stein used in some versions.[1] I call Stein's tautology mischievous because it is self-problematizing. Its emphatic reduplication not only interrogates the facility of such metaphoric clichés as "my love is a rose." It calls attention to the increasingly nontautological potency of the repeated identity phrases in "a rose is [not] a rose is [not] a rose."

Frost's initial word announces the difference that is the theme of the poem: "The" particular or unique or archetypal rose is a rose—only an individual, an instance, a member of a class. The secret, or trick, in the poem is that there exists a large family of herbs, shrubs, and trees—115 genera—that bear the name *rosaceae*.[2] Since apple, pear, and plum belong to that family, they are called "rose" by metonymic transfer from family to species. Once we know this, we become uncertain whether "the rose is a rose" is a tautology or a metonymy. The speaker says, "the theory now goes," to remind us that the difference in the character of the trope is an effect of the history of classification.

This particular speaker has his feet on the ground. Like a good, simple, but shrewd country cousin, he pretends not to have much respect for the way those clever city fellers, the scientists and classifiers, try to bamboozle us with newfangled inventions for complexifying and redefining the world. Their categories are clearly fictions. They defy common sense. They mess up such self-evident truths and certain certainties as the principle of identity, the difference between apples and pears, and the poetic clichés of lovers.

Frost doesn't make the genre of this poem explicit until the last two lines: a love poem addressed to "You"—his friend? His beloved? Its tone is radically affected by "of course": "naturally; this is what I'm expected to say. Let's minimize the cost of the sentimentality that always undoes this genre."

The speaker's concluding variation on the old favorite, "my love is a rose," rehabilitates it as the kind of assured and assuring fiction that's worth holding on to. Its value—the value embedded in his ironic "of course"—lies in its being so patently a metaphoric fiction.

Even though time and custom have diminished the force of the contradictory ("you were never a rose"), it can be reanimated by being redirected, as it is now, through the saying of this poem and in an ironically subdued profession of love. At the same time, the metonymic reality of classification is rendered suspect: No less fictitious than poetry, it nevertheless imposes itself on life in the imperial mode of scientific ideology, a mode that tries to reduce the relations between persons to the status of mere metaphoric fantasies.

Frost writes as a reluctant modernist—that is, as someone who is urbanely skeptical even as he disapproves of modernity's pursuit of disenchantment. But he stages this critique from the blinkered position of the pastoral or rural traditionalist. This allows him simultaneously to appropriate the wisdom of the backwoods speakers he so often ventriloquizes and to distance himself from their reductiveness.

Diffused but still audible, still legible, in the plaintive nostalgia of those speakers is Frost's (and modernism's) major insight into the irreversible consequence of the world's disenchantment: Our linguistic habits, our figures of speech and thought, our systems of signification and reference, have always constituted the transcendent realities that both enshrine our ideals and affect our behavior. So, for example, the elegiac speaker in "The White-Tailed Hornet" (a poem subtitled "The Revision of Theories") laments that

> Our worship, humor, conscientiousness
> Went long since to the dogs under the table.
> And served us right for having instituted
> Downward comparisons. As long on earth
> As our comparisons were stoutly upward
> With gods and angels, we were men at least,
> But little lower than the gods and angels.
> But once comparisons were yielded downward,
> Once we began to see our images
> Reflected in the mud and even dust,

'Twas disillusion upon disillusion.
We were lost piecemeal to the animals,
Like people thrown out to delay the wolves.

This complaint provides me with my cue to go back in time in order to explore comparisons that were so stoutly upward they seemed to many to be not mere comparisons but realities.

PART II

History

EIGHT

Metaphor and the Anxiety of Fictiveness: St. Augustine

Some of my previous remarks may suggest that our basic human impulse to metonymize or demetaphorize attained to its most triumphant moment in the Christian culture of the High Middle Ages. There if anywhere the unconscious and mechanical prejudices of language and perception were most fully reinforced by the flowering of a highly sophisticated and articulate cultural consciousness fashioned in the same mode and shaped by the same prejudices. But this is just what needs to be questioned.

Coming back to the Middle Ages from our standpoint beyond the End of Western Metaphysics, we discover something very different, and the hypothesis I'm about to test is this: Demetaphorizing and metonymizing best serve their adaptive functions by remaining unconscious—remaining what sociologists call latent or unintended functions. If they become manifest (intended) functions, then they become latent dysfunctions.

For medieval culture latency is itself functional and manifestness dysfunctional. Latency is a latent function. When these processes are taken up at the level of conscious activity, when they become culturally approved and encouraged, they jeopardize the very structure of order and redundancy they are trying to sustain, and they jeopardize it by the very fact that they—as conscious processes—are delegated to preserve it. In the discussion that follows I'll outline St. Augustine's response to this problem.

Charles Singleton's epigrammatic remark that the "fiction of the *Divine Comedy* is that it is not a fiction" provides a compact entry into our topic.[1] As Singleton and others have shown, Dante seemed aware of the presumptuousness of the claim and tried to defuse it.[2] But the awareness of danger was already present in St. Augustine, and I begin with a quick sketch of his peculiar and brilliant effort to deploy metaphor and metonymy in a dialectical configuration that would keep the human creature from the extremes of presumptuousness and impotent despair.

In chapter 5 I quoted a sentence from Margaret Ferguson's essay on St. Augustine's linguistic theory and practice, and I now want to return to that brilliant study. Ferguson explores the "striking parallel between the situation of exile, the persona banished from his proper place to an alien one," and Cicero's definition of metaphorical words as "those which are transferred and placed, as it were, in an alien place."[3] Since for St. Augustine, the human creature's proper place is the Heavenly City, and since language, like the creature, is exiled from the eternity of the one (an infinity of presence) to the perpetuity of the many (an infinity of sequence), it follows that "all language is a metaphorical detour in the road to God because no sequence of words, even 'proper' words, can adequately represent an atemporal and holistic significance" (844).

Ferguson argues that when St. Augustine uses "spatial terms whose literal denotation he would reject" it is to suggest a fundamental linguistic flaw, "something in the nature of language which necessitates a spatial understanding of a difference—an unlikeness—that is not spatial . . . at all" (853). And this holds not only for the spatializing of moral unlikeness as distance, but also for the tendency to describe temporal phenomena in terms of linear extension. By an Eleatic process of subdivision, St. Augustine reduces the units of time to nonexistence, shows them up as "fictional denominations," and discovers that since "the present has no space" and is unextended, "the terms which designate the 'present' are necessarily figural because the present is literally absent" (854–55). Temporality vanishes into nothing when we try to grasp it with language, for "all referents other than God are constituted by 'not-being'" (856). Language is thus radically figurative in two ways, one necessitated by the ontological transcendence of the referent, the other by the "ontological absence" of the referent.

In this radical perspective there is either God or there is nothing. Everything between is the fictive constitution by fallen humans of their home away from home: self-incarceration in the prisonhouse of language and perception. All the evolutionary adaptations by which human perception had stabilized and domesticated experience in order to diminish the terror of temporality and strangeness are hereby thrown into question. St. Augustine reaches deep beneath the homelike sediment with which our canny nature has shielded itself. He aims to touch and startle into life once again the most profound anxieties, and to alienate us from the world we have made. What could be more modern than this remetaphorizing project?

But despite the similarity of structure, St. Augustine's project differs drastically in mode and response. His discovery of the fictive and illusory character of earthly existence is not directed toward increasing human control over it: Our constitutive power is our weakness, the mark of our fallibility. This, however, isn't St. Augustine's only theory, even if it's the one that seems to dominate the *Confessions*. We have to add another formulation to Ferguson's, for St. Augustine is also one of the great metonymizers of the Western tradition.

Under the aegis of the phrase, "Deus creator omnium," he begins to reconstruct the order of mere perpetuity into the ever widening network of contained and containing parts (described in *Confessions* 11.28) that binds "the lives of all" into a community. And here, as in the cosmological nest of spheres that it so interestingly resembles, the possibility arises of a more positive metonymic figuration by which the part can symbolize the whole, the effect the cause, the lower the higher, and the visible the invisible. The term "symbolize" in this context means not merely "stand for." It has a more dynamic and complex meaning: "to reach toward" and "to fall short of."

From the modern standpoint, this positive figuration is no less metaphoric than the negative figuration Ferguson discusses. But to St. Augustine the difference is profound. In *City of God* 13.21 he criticizes those who "allegorize all that concerns Paradise itself, where the first men, the parents of the human race, are, according to the truth of holy Scripture, recorded to have been"; those allegorizers "understand all its trees and fruit-bearing plants as virtues and habits of life, as if they had no existence in the external world, but were only so spoken of or related for the sake of spiritual meanings. As if there could not be a real terrestrial paradise!"

The danger here is that the garden God made will be less real than the meanings his creatures arbitrarily read into it. In Dante's terms, the danger is that the referents of the literal level of Scripture will become metaphoric vehicles in an allegory of poets. This danger can be avoided by accentuating the typological or figural level of allegory. As we learn in Book 12 of the *Confessions*, God created spiritual and visible referents and meanings together. The aim of St. Augustine's strategy in this twelfth book seems to be to limit the power of any one human interpreter, and to safeguard the rich multifold truth of Scripture. But the very personal interpretation he gives of Genesis in Book 13—in which he elicits from Scripture the meaning that validates the unique experience of the *Confessions*—retrospectively converts Book 12 to an anticipatory apologia.

In assimilating both his experience and his novel effort at autobiography to the biblical paradigm, doesn't he at the same time reduce the paradigm to an ancillary subtext that confers its authority on his own text? Is there any slippage from "*Confessions* is like Genesis" to "*Confessions* is a genesis"? Doesn't Genesis come close to being little more than a metaphoric amplifier for personal conversion, for new birth, for a new beginning?

It isn't easy for St. Augustine to maintain in tensional equilibrium the opposed processes of metaphor and metonymy. Metaphorizing, the radical fictionalizing of space-time, is not likely to cause much trouble, for several reasons. First, because it contradicts the prejudices of perception, prejudices that had adaptively evolved for eons toward an ideal of security, familiarity, predictability, simplification, domestication—an ideal, in short, of comfortable over-order. Second, because metaphorizing could be validated only by the norms of modern culture, with its acceptance of radical human creativity and of the counterperceptual character of physical reality. From the modern standpoint, medieval culture would later regress to what is superficially a more primitive vision by embracing a cosmology that upheld perception and its urge to over-order. Third, because St. Augustine believed in the need to work for Christian community in this world. The de-realizing performed by metaphor made it harder to take the world seriously enough to be able to commit oneself to it. The Christian realist in St. Augustine, as in the later Middle Ages, acknowledges this by leaning heavily on the metonymizing process in order to dignify historical and political experience by connecting them to higher levels of reality.

Finally, we might entertain a more psychological explanation: The radical nature of metaphor could be seen as a violent recoil from the other extreme, a recoil in which St. Augustine devalues what he finds dangerously appealing. His prose conveys his sense of mastery over the resources of rhetorical art, and conveys at the same time his dialectical awareness that those resources, that mastery, could, by their very richness and power, undo him. Medieval culture looks back over its shoulder not toward primitive culture but toward Hellenistic and Roman classicism, toward the brilliant and terrifying image of the failure of human art at its most powerful.

The failure of the City of Man and its civilization was a clear message that the city had to be removed from human hands and led back to God if its accomplishments were to be salvaged. Yet Rome couldn't simply be obliterated from Christian consciousness. It lingered on in too many forms—institutions, customs, monuments, ruins, roads, laws, and texts—that were not easy to ignore or condemn.

Christian culture could use and enjoy the resources of Rome only if it made an effort to displace from consciousness the awareness of human power that was the fruit of the Roman experience. What jeopardized this project of displacement and revision from the beginning was its mode of expression. It could hardly present itself in the mode of primitive ejaculation or automatic writing. It had to be a fully conscious enterprise based on historical criticism and employing the most highly developed instruments of art and technique—the instruments of thought and action bequeathed by classical culture. And although this was a contradiction in terms, it produced a culture that for centuries sustained, not a stagnant "medieval synthesis," but a dynamic interaction, a precarious and ever-changing equilibrium, between divine transcendence and human art.

In differentiating and equilibrating the two figural modes, St. Augustine displayed prophetic awareness of the dangers posed by the specter of the deconstructive operation Kenneth Burke called *logology* in his study of the rhetoric of religion. Logology involves a double reduction. It reduces the study of God first to the study of "words about God" and then to "studies in words-about-words."[4]

St. Augustine responded to these dangers with a tensional solution that was taken up again and again by subsequent Christian thinkers. But it was a necessarily flawed solution. He recognized that metaphorizing is an express exile from reality. But it isn't clear that he recognized the metonymic process as a covert escape from fiction.

Remember that the lurking metaphoric negation, the "A is not B" behind the assertion "A is B," makes any metaphoric coupling fictive or counterfactual. Metonymizing suppresses the negation in order to disclaim metaphor's origin in the human mind and displace it to God. Medieval thought always rode uneasily on this necessary suppression because it was often difficult to suppress the awareness of suppression. The degree of awareness and uneasiness varied with the nature of the enterprise. In the next chapter I discuss three different kinds of medieval project, taken more or less in the order of increasing uneasiness: first, a gloss on the book of Genesis from Hugh of St. Victor's instructional work on the sacraments of the Christian faith; second, Abbott Suger's building and writing project in connection with St. Denis (with a brief look at his contemporary, St. Bernard); finally, Dante's *Divine Comedy*. As you can probably guess in advance, the increasing uneasiness will be connected to the increasingly self-assertive role played by human creation.

NINE

Metaphor and Metonymy in the Middle Ages: Aquinas and Dante

The time is the late Middle Ages. The texts that follow illustrate the kinds of historical constraint that impose themselves on the characterization and valuation of our two rhetorical figures. The first passage, a famous anonymous jingle, states in popular form the theory of fourfold interpretation that guides much symbolic practice during the Christian Middle Ages, and the second passage is an equally famous but sophisticated justification of the theory:

1. Littera gesta docet
quid credas, allegoria
moralia, quid ages,
quod tendas, anagogia.

(The letter teaches deeds; the allegory, what you should believe; the moral [or tropological level] what you should do; the anagoge [mystical level] whither you should direct your course [in the next life].)

2. The author of Holy Writ is God, in whose power it is to signify His meaning, not by words only (as man also can do), but also by things themselves. So whereas in every other science things are signified by words, this science [sacred science, i.e., theology] has the property that the things signified by the words have themselves also a signification. Therefore that first signification whereby words signify things belongs to the first sense, the historical or literal. That signification whereby things . . . have themselves also a signification is called the spiritual sense, which is based on the literal and presupposes it.[1]

The most obvious function performed by this theory is to guarantee the transcendence of reality to language. As Aquinas defines it, the literal level refers simultaneously to all four preexisting and preverbal levels of reality—the historical, the typological or figural, the tropological or moral, and the anagogical or mystical. These levels are arranged to allow language to move metonymically back and forth between or among them.

3. Luce ed amore d'un cerchio lui comprende,
si come questo li altri, e quel precinto
colui che 'l cinge solamente intende.
(Dante, *Paradiso*, 27.112–14)

(Light and love comprehend it in one circle, just as this [sphere comprehends] the others, and he who bounds it alone understands that containment.)

4. . . . come il tempo tegna in cotal testo
le sue radici e ne li altri le fronde,
omai a te può esser manifesto.
(*Paradiso*, 27.118–20)

(how time may have in that container [*testo*, literally, flowerpot] its roots, and in the others its leaves, can now be clear to you.)

In passage 3, the "it" ("lui") comprehended by light and love is the Primum Mobile, the ninth and outermost of the spheres revolving around the earth in Dante's variation of what Thomas Kuhn calls the basic "two-sphere" model of the geocentric universe that underlies Aristotelian cosmology and Ptolemaic astronomy.[2] It is necessary to know this in order to grasp the context of passage 4: "The unit of time is the day, which is determined by the revolution of the Primum Mobile." The Primum Mobile transmits its "motion to the other spheres" contained within it, and it is this "total revolution" that "makes time."[3] Thus time is a plant that has its roots in the Primum Mobile and grows downward through the spheres toward the center.

We recognize this without hesitation as strong metaphor. The metaphoric negation (time is not a plant) clearly throws us into higher interpretive gear. And yet once we've puzzled over the figure and explained it to ourselves, we may find that it wants to be resolved into an interrelated series of weak metaphors and metonymic statements about the origins of time in the revolutions of the ninth sphere. But the context and moral valency of the two passages are qualified by the fact that both are marked as Beatrice's utterances to the pilgrim. They precede her harsh tirade against human greed.

The flowerpot figure is part of a set of oppositional images in which time intermingled with *virtù* rains down ("l'amor . . . la virtù . . . piove," 27.111) from this sphere like grace only to be countered and challenged by another kind of downpour: the waves of cupidity that rot the human will. The "continual rain" of greed spoils "sound plums . . . so that the human family goes astray" until a time in the future when "good fruit shall follow the flower" (*Par.* 27.121–48). Such figures are marked as patterns of simile-like weak metaphor in which flowing and growing downward mimetically represent a conflict of "real" forces operating across the vertical ranges of the geocentric universe.

In the *Convivio,* Dante gives both a historical and a technical or "scientific" account of the universe depicted in his poem. To justify certain motions left unexplained by the Aristotelian eight-sphere model, Ptolemy postulates the existence and dynamic agency of the *primum mobile,* which "is called by many the crystalline heaven, that is, the diaphanous, or all-transparent." Beyond all these, Dante continues, "Catholics assert the empyrean heaven, which is as much as to say the heaven of flame, or the luminous heaven; and they assert it to be immovable, because it has in itself, with respect to every part, that which its matter requires."

The empyrean is "the place of that supreme deity which alone completely perceives itself." It is "the place of the blessed spirits" and "the sovereign edifice of the world, wherein all the world is enclosed, and outside of which is nothing; and it is not itself in space, but was formed only in the primal mind."[4] Material, spiritual, spatial, and nonspatial, components are strangely interwoven in a dense-to-rare schema. As the "dwelling" of immaterial substances—God, saints, and angels—the empyrean is the container of the spatial universe yet somehow not spatial. It provides a setting in which spiritual states and directions can attain to virtually literal topicality. Its order confers predictability and pattern, and encourages the visualization of hierarchy and correspondences.

In this passage, Dante "charts the position . . . of God's abode" neither as a poet nor as a mathematician but as an "astronomer" and "theologian."[5] His account is not presented as a patently poetic fiction. He doesn't offer it as one of the hypothetical explanations invented by mathematicians who use such dubious entities as epicycles, deferents, and eccentrics to explain observed facts and thus to save the appearances. Rather, he presents his account as a description.[6] The credibility of any datum as an "observed fact" is itself contingent on the rhetorical and grammatical form in which it is expressed. Description as an indicative mode is a constitutive speech act. What it constitutes is an intention not to constitute but to refer, an intention to point to and to register—literally, to write down—something already "out there in nature."

If that referent happens to be a displaced or projected cultural phantasm, then description pretends to a specious transparency: It pretends only to indicate what in fact it creates or re-creates. Such acts of displacement to nature were continuously reproduced and stabilized by mechanisms of transmission that were as prestigious as they were unreliable. For centuries, the questionable origins of many discourses—in fiction, myth, hypothesis, conjecture, faulty induction, and overemphasis on syllogistic reasoning—were not only muffled and ignored or forgotten. They were also preserved by the accidents and mistakes (scribal errors, fragmented texts, glossarial fantasies, and the like) attendant on the interpretive power vested in pretypographic practices of writing and reading.[7]

Confidence in this textual machinery nevertheless gives Dante permission not only to describe the empyrean but also to explain that it transcends reason because, while it is the container of the physical universe, it somehow is not physical but purely spiritual. It is the divine mind as "place," but the relation of this mystical term "place" to physical "place" is not metaphoric. It is closer to metonymic because the two kinds of place are bound together by a more general concept of containment in which they ontologically participate and of which they are logically parts. This is why the light and love, *luce ed amore,* of passage 3 are literal: the subtle light of the empyrean (see passage 5 below), and the divine love with which God encircles and sustains his world.

Given the scientifico-religious reality of the empyrean, it's easy to understand why Dante's reference to "the heaven of flame, or the luminous heaven" is no metaphor. Nevertheless, the account seems to swerve more than once toward metaphoric fantasy, as in this example: "the cause of the primum mobile having the swiftest motion . . . [is] the most fervid appetite wherewith every part of this ninth heaven . . . longs to be conjoined with every part of this most divine and tranquil heaven, [and] it revolves therein with so great yearning that its swiftness is scarce to be comprehended."[8] To modern readers it may seem that since the primum mobile itself is not conscious, it cannot have appetites and longings. Dante must therefore be using a metaphor to describe the speed and power with which it turns. Yet this isn't so, not merely because Aristotle (and others) assigned souls to the spheres. It isn't so because the terms of appetite and aspiration belong to an anthropomorphic but ostensively scientific discourse that dates back through Aristotle's *Physics* to the mythopoetic speculations of such Pre-Socratic authors as Empedocles.

This discourse uses a lexicon that attributes phenomena of gravitation to a form of natural appetite based on the attraction of like things. Heavy things tend down toward (are attracted to, long for) the center while light things tend upward.[9] As with the principle of containment mentioned above, the principle of attraction is the most general concept, and it subdivides into the attraction, or appetite, of inanimate and animate beings. Dante's terms may have an edge of metaphoric enhancement but they are fundamentally metonymic.

One of the factors contributing to the metonymic and referential force of Dante's terms was, as I noted, the naturalizing effect of transmission mechanisms that were as prestigious as they were unreliable. Aquinas was a relatively recent beneficiary and enforcer of the Aristotelian cosmology that sustained and was in turn sustained by the tradition of Christian realism. The mystery Dante discusses in the *Convivio* passage and alludes to in the final words of passage 3 ("colui che il cinge solamente intende": only God "understands/ intends that containment") is also glanced at in the final, carefully noncommital, sentence in passage 5:

> 5. But since the body of the firmament, although solid, is nevertheless transparent, since it does not exclude light, as is clear from this, [i.e.] that we see the stars unobstructed by the intervening heavens, it may also be said that the empyrean heaven has light, not condensed so as to emit rays, as the body of the sun does, but more subtle. Or it could have the brightness of glory, which is not the same as natural brightness.[10]

"Or it could have the brightness of glory": an air of indistinctness allows Aquinas to affirm the transcendence of spiritual reality and at the same time makes it hard to conceive of this reality as extricable from its spatial model. The long first sentence is meant as literal statement, for it asserts what is believed to be physical or astronomical truth.

Like Dante after him, Aquinas encourages the reader to take for granted the scientific reality of the crystalline spheres and the quintessence, and to think of them as in some way part of the *visibilia* that perception delivers to the mind. Indeed, even the verb, "patet" ("is clear, evident, apparent"), which is casually used as a phrasal connector in the first sentence, insinuates the perceptual order into the grammar of explanation. By the time we reach the final sentence, we have been persuaded that although the perceptual image of glory falls short of its referent, the difference between them may itself be comparative rather than absolute. It may be a difference of physico-perceptual degree in the dense-to-rare spectrum: Natural light is less "subtilem," less finely—more coarsely—spun and thus less rarefied; it is "condensatam," very dense or thick.[11]

Belief in the reality of this cosmos—belief that it was created by God, not by Aristotle—makes it possible to embed mystical doctrine in the objective structure of the world and thereby to fend off metaphoric reductions of sacred universal truth to pious personal fancies. Just as physical and mystical categories of place are correlated to distinguish corresponding parts of the real world, so different kinds of sight or vision and their object—different kinds of light or brightness—are correlated in a metonymic relationship. Any term, Aquinas insists, "may be employed in two senses, one in accordance with its first imposition, the other with common usage [*usum nominis*]." Thus the term "vision" that is first used "to signify the act of the sense of sight . . . is extended in common usage [*extensum . . .secundum usum loquentium*] to the cognition of the other senses . . . and even beyond that to the cognition of the intellect,"

> 6. and the same may be said of the name "light." For it was first instituted to signify that which makes manifest to the sense of sight; afterwards it was extended to the signifying of all that makes manifest to cognition of any kind.
>
> If therefore the name "light" is taken in the sense first imposed, it may be ascribed [dicitur] metaphorically to spiritual things. . . . But if in accordance with common usage it is extended to manifestation of every kind, it may properly be ascribed to spiritual things.[12]

In other words, if we were to explain this in terms of the simple antithetical model of literal versus figurative meaning, we would say that strictly literal usage refers to perceptual experience of the real world, while metaphor is its contrary. Metaphor is a mental construct involving a transfer of one part of the cosmic order to another in a relation that is understood not to correspond to anything in the reality beyond the mind. If a term properly signifies only one referent and is thus univocal, when it is "used of anything else, it is used metaphorically and . . . improperly."[13] A is B, but not really: "Things said metaphorically do not retain the same concept . . . but only the same name"; therefore "the terms used in metaphorical analogies . . . are merely given an analogical reference by the mind."[14] They are no more than epistemic fantasies.

But this simple rhetorical model wasn't the only available ratio. The idea of metaphoric transfer could be replaced or supplemented by that of extension, in which a referent in one sector of the universe is linked to a referent in another sector in a relationship that *does*, according to belief, correspond to something in the reality beyond the mind. The three principles to which Dante and Aquinas appeal in the passages discussed above—containment, attraction, and manifestation—are treated as ontological modes and not merely as analytic or epistemological categories. They distinguish and interrelate different parts of the universe in terms of parallelism, hierarchy, and causality. If they initially appeared as discursive suppositions or posits, usage transformed them first into prediscursive presuppositions and then into deposits.[15]

The epistemological rationale that accommodates this alternative model derives ultimately from Aristotle's *De Anima* and medieval commentaries on it, and it may be profiled as follows. The object of perception is perceived as a datum, a given. Perception perceives itself as passively, therefore accurately, registering the sensibilia it receives from the outside. Any constructs, theoretical objects, or hypothetical entities that are devised to "save appearances" and that are packed into percepts through acculturation are thereby naturalized—transformed into passively received data. If they are received as *invisibilia* in a mode that might be characterized as "*visibilia*, but not really," the formula doesn't pack its metaphoric and fictive punch. Rather, unlike metaphor, which is countervisual, we're encouraged to look on *visibilia* as images and copies of—clues to—the *invisibilia* to which they are correlated. This makes the *invisibilia* ghostly images or copies of the *visibilia* they supposedly resemble.[16] The structure of such analogies is perfectly described by the definition of the trope *denominatio* cited in chapter 2 from Lewis and Short's *Latin Dictionary:* "the substitution of the name of an object for that of another to which it has some relation, as the name of the cause for that of the effect, of the property for that of the substance, etc.; a metonymy."

Such an alternative to metaphoricity is produced by putting into play a perspectival antithesis between the *ordo nominis* (the order of knowing, naming, signifying) and the *ordo rerum* (the order of things). Thus, as Ralph McInerny notes, Aquinas argues that the term "light . . . is first assigned to signify a notion expressing something in the sensible order, that which makes bodies visible, and this is its *ratio propria,*" which "involves matter, for it refers to the external sense." There is also, however, "a common notion (*ratio communis*) signified by the term . . . 'principle of manifestation.'" Since this term "contains no reference to matter," it may be used to signify "spiritual things":

> What is more, the term which then signifies spiritual things, does so more properly than it does corporeal things. . . . If usage indicates that the meaning of the name has been extended, . . . the spiritual principle of manifestation . . . is really or ontologically more perfect than the sun. This scale of priority and posteriority is secondum ordinem rerum.[17]

Extension, then, is the metonymic alternative to metaphor. It is an analogical mean between the univocal and equivocal extremes.

In this view, metaphor is a technique for neither the discovery nor the constitution of reality. It is relegated to limited uses as a rhetorical, decorative, or heuristic device—for example, to help accommodate transcendent reality to the limited capacities of mortals, or to encourage them to stretch their minds beyond the visible toward the invisible. "When Scripture speaks of God's arm, the literal sense is not that God has such a member, but only what is signified by this member, namely, operative power" (*S.T.*, I, 10, ad 3).

By displaying its inadequacy, the figure leads the mind beyond this visual or sensible image toward the spiritual truth about God's power. The use of conspicuously inadequate metaphors is "befitting the knowledge of God that we have in this life. For what He is not is clearer to us than what He is" (*S.T.*, I, 9, ad 3).

> Thomas discusses the fact that metaphor, which seems to be a device distinctive of poetry and foreign to the physical and mathematical sciences and to metaphysics and logic, turns up time and again in Christian theology. . . .
>
> The science of poetry is about things which because of their deficiency of truth cannot be laid hold of by the reason; hence the reason has to be drawn off to the side by means of certain comparisons. But then, theology is about things which lie beyond reason. Thus the symbolic method is common to both sciences, since neither is of itself accommodated [to human reason]. . . .

> For Thomas, Christian theology and poetry are indeed not the same thing, but lie at opposite poles of human knowledge. However, the very fact that they are opposite extremes gives them something of a common relation to that which lies between them: they both operate on the periphery of human intellection.[18]

The difference between poetry and theology is precisely that between metaphor and metonymy. Yet notice that Aquinas's explanation of "God's arm" bends it toward the metonymic status of, say, "the pen" as a symbol of literary power. And there is an interesting strain in the passage: The recognition that "the symbolic method is common to both sciences" is coupled with the need to emphasize that they "lie at opposite poles of human knowledge." I sense something like an ideological pressure to sustain that emphasis against the prior recognition. I note above that a metonymic transfer "does, according to belief, correspond to something in the reality outside the mind," and it is now time to confess that the qualifier "according to belief" may not be as casual as it seemed. In fact, it may threaten the very distinction I'm trying to uphold between metaphor and metonymy.

Here, then, is the problem in a nutshell: If you take away that spherical Aristotelian cosmos—or take away belief in its transcendent or God-made reality—metonymies turn into metaphors. The inference to be drawn from this is that the two must have the same intrinsic logico-syntactic or rhetorical structure, and that what distinguishes any such structure as metaphoric or metonymic lies outside the study of rhetorical figures in itself. Whether we see any analogy, correspondence, or transfer of names as metaphoric or as metonymic, will depend on what we believe to be actual and real, on what we believe to be imaginary.

This means not only that the identification of any rhetorical structure as one or the other, as metaphor or as metonymy, will be culturally conditioned. It also means that we have to go beyond linguistic, rhetorical, and semantic analysis into cultural and historical inquiry in order to define the status and limits of the metaphoric over against whatever is nonmetaphoric. If the difference between metaphor and metonymy rests on the strength or weakness of the contradictory, "A is B / A is not B," it can't rest on a closed logical structure because the force of the contradictory is conditioned by cultural influence.

TEN

Sacramental Anxiety in the Late Middle Ages: Hugh of St. Victor, the Abbot Suger, and Dante

The following is a passage from Hugh of St. Victor's treatise, *On the Sacraments of the Christian Faith.* Born in Saxony in 1096, Hugh spent most of his life in Paris, and when he died in 1141 he had been the successful head of the monastery school of St. Victor for eight years.

> Et ut mihi videtur eodem prorsus temporis momento quo visibiliter et corporaliter divisa est lux a tenebris; invisibiliter quoque boni angeli discreti sunt a malis illis in tenebras peccati cadentibus: et istis ad lucem justitiae conversis illuminatisque a luce, ut lux essent et non tenebrae. *Sic enim consonare debuerunt exemplaria operum Dei, ut quae visibilia erant opera sapientiae, invisibilium proventus sequerentur, secundum quod ipsa quae utrobique operabatur sapientia, ibi judicium exercuit, hic formavit exemplum.*[1]

> And at the very moment when light was visibly and corporeally separated from darkness, the good angels were invisibly set apart

> from the wicked angels who were falling in the darkness of sin. The good were illumined and converted to the light of righteousness, that they might be light and not darkness. *Thus we ought to perceive a consonance in the works of God, the visible work conforming to the tissue of the invisible in such wise that the Wisdom which worked in both may in the former instruct by example and in the latter execute judgment.*[2]

The translator's rendering of the passage is generally permissive, and since his treatment of the italicized passage is loose to the point of inaccuracy, I supply two alternatives:

> And in my opinion, at exactly the same moment of time at which light was divided visibly and corporeally from darkness, invisibly also the good angels were separated from those evil angels who were falling into the darkness of sin; the former too being turned toward the light of justice and illumined by the light, that they might be light and not darkness. *For thus the exemplars of God's works had to be in harmony, so that those works of wisdom which were visible might follow the products of the invisible, according as this wisdom itself, operating in both cases, in the one exercised judgment, in the other formed an example.*[3]

> And as it seems to me, in that very moment of time when light was visibly and corporeally divided from darkness, the good angels were also invisibly set apart from the wicked angels who were falling into the darkness of sin; and the former were turned toward the light of justice and illuminated by the light, so that they might be light and not darkness. *Thus the patterns of God's works were obliged to be harmonious so that those which were visible works of wisdom should follow the happy outcome [proventus] of invisible things in such a manner that the wisdom which worked in both exercised judgment there [in dividing the angels], fashioned an example here [in the firmament].*[4]

Our view of the extent of Hugh's interference is likely to differ from his. To us it may seem that the visible qualities of light and dark are transferred to the spiritual order by Hugh rather than by God. And to us the visible work may appear to be the original while the invisible work is a copy figuratively derived from the visible order by the metaphoric transfers, "virtue is light" and "sin is darkness." But Hugh could object that his gloss has the authority of a long tradition dating back at least to St. Augustine, and he would have been supported by St. Thomas Aquinas, who treated such transfers as examples of extension, or metonymy.

In J.-P. Migne's *Patrologia Latina* this passage follows almost eight columns of natural philosophy (187A–194B) in which Hugh tries to develop a scientifico-literal explanation of the opening verses of Genesis. The aim of the whole discussion is its moral application to the light of virtue and the darkness of sin in the soul (I.i.xii). Extending his account of the cosmos to the microcosm, Hugh patterns it after the Pauline and Augustinian formula, "that was first which was fleshly, afterwards that which is spiritual"; "no one will be good who was not first of all wicked." Thus he begins chapter xii by asserting that "every soul so long as it is in sin is so to speak [*quasi*] in a kind of [*quibusdam*] darkness and confusion." It cannot "be given the order and form of righteousness" unless it first becomes conscious of its own evil—unless it "distinguishes the light from the darkness, that is, the virtues from the vices," and unless it "disposes itself to order, and conforms itself to truth" (*PL*, 176, 195C). The soul can best do this by studying the literal and spiritual senses of scripture, for all the works of the first three days of Genesis exhibit spiritual patterns (196B).

This study is in fact what Hugh has been urging the soul to pursue. He opens on a reflexive note that models the proper attitude toward the inquiry: *ut mihi videtur* casually and modestly dramatizes the role of an instructor who approaches God's lessons as a learner. The human learning process is implicitly contrasted to the speedy and early conversion of the good angels. Hugh affirms the fallibility, the limited perspective, of a *magister* who is himself still working to dispose his soul to order and conform it to truth.

The instructional context probably accounts for Taylor's mistranslation of *consonare debuerunt,* and even confers a certain rightness on it, because it increases the vaguely self-conscious or self-referring character of the gloss. "Thus we ought to perceive a consonance"—and Hugh is now perceiving a consonance. Yet the thought that Taylor's rendering is dramatically appropriate increases the significance of Hugh's passing it up. For instead of moral exhortation by the interpreter in the present moment ("we ought to perceive"), the tense and person and number of *debuerunt* indicates a response that was fully determined by divine fiat at the beginning of time ("they had to harmonize").

This reminds us that it was God, not Hugh, who made the initial moral judgment that prefigures the happy outcome of the Last Judgment. It was God who shaped the natural alternations of day and night that utter the ongoing conflict between good and bad spiritual powers. It was God who created ontological figures and tropes and who made the letter follow its spiritual exemplar in a harmony that was both visible in nature and audible in the voices of scripture.

In this fashion Hugh certifies the transcendent source of his metonymies and justifies the need for an interpreter. Because God has made the world safe for metonymy, the interpreter is not merely *enabled* to declare them. He is *obliged* to declare them. Hugh's act of elaborating the correspondence is at the same time a disclaimer of metaphor—of creative responsibility—on his part.

But it isn't a very strong disclaimer, and my picking away at the passage hasn't turned up a great deal of ontological insecurity. Only when we set it in a larger context does the apologetic edge of self-awareness become less faint. Hugh was active in a time of great ferment and controversy. It was the time of Abelard and his *Sic et Non,* the time of the Abbott Suger, his politics, and his abbey church of St. Denis, the time of St. Bernard and his criticism of the vanity and curiosity of human art, and the time of the interest in classical cosmologies promoted at Chartres.

In Beryl Smalley's words, Hugh's project was "to recall rebellious learning back to the scriptural framework."[5] Jerome Taylor has persuasively shown how Hugh displayed his awareness of the problem of interpretation by including and subtly altering a variety of heterodox materials. "By using them," Taylor remarks, "Hugh spoke to his contemporaries in terms significant in their times; by adapting their meaning, he made them promote a point of view actually alien . . . to the borrowed texts themselves, and hence gave, even to those who might disagree with him, an attractive proof of ingenuity."[6]

Taylor argues that this ingenuity was evident in the *Didascalicon* as a whole, for the work was "original in its own time" as well as "in relation to traditional Christian didascalic works."[7] Its orientation is "toward the restoration within the individual lector . . . of the image of the divine Wisdom."[8] A major aspect of Hugh's originality lies in what Taylor describes as his ability to adapt "currently fashionable cosmological texts and themes" to his analysis of the progress by which the learner could achieve that goal of spiritual restoration.[9] Hugh depicts the learner's pursuit of the image through knowledge and virtue as an ascent spatially reinforced by the cosmographic scheme of the medieval universe, with its hierarchy of concentric spheres. The close interweaving of its sub- and superlunary regions with the visible and invisible worlds provides a setting that enables Hugh to sustain analogies of enlightenment and ascent in the realist mode of metonymy rather than in the fictive mode of metaphor.

This was an age that teemed with conflicting interpretations, all of them claiming an insider's access to God's mind and meanings. The need to write a *Didascalicon* reveals the seriousness of this problem. But Hugh's ingenuity and originality may well have re-created the problem he intended to solve. Of this he could hardly be unaware, and in the *Didascalicon* he directs a warning to others. One or two points of this warning he—or someone else—could as easily have applied to himself:

> You see that many who read Scriptures, because they do not have a foundation of truth, fall into various errors and change their views almost as often as they sit down to read. But you see others who, in accordance with that knowledge of the truth upon which, interiorly, they are solidly based, know how to bend all Scriptural passages whatever into fitting interpretations and to judge both what is out of keeping with sound faith and what is consonant with it. . . . But I do not say these things in order to offer anyone the chance to interpret the Scriptures according to his own will, but in order to show the man who follows the letter alone that he cannot long continue without error. For this reason it is necessary both that we follow the letter in such a way as not to prefer our own sense to the divine author's, and that we do not follow it in such a way as to deny that the entire pronouncement of truth is rendered in it.[10]

Such methodological statements betray an insecurity that is not eccentric or arbitrary but inherent in and kept alive by the basic situation of Christian medieval culture.

Elsewhere, Hugh finds it necessary to condemn "the disputes of men who, out of vain curiosity, pry into the hidden things of God's works" and make up "lies about things of which they are ignorant."[11] The necessity to condemn suggests to me that the difference between lies and truth is something to be decided by the human arts of persuasion in the courtroom of one's human peers and successors. No matter who is undertaking to defend divine truth, the very act of defense—since defense becomes appropriation—threatens to demystify the truth and expose it as a human lie for others to condemn. And the more brilliantly the advocate represents his divine client, the more he endangers his client's (and therefore his own) legitimacy.

This problem of divine advocacy becomes more pressing when what is at issue is something more tangible and immediate, more communal and public, than a text. Consider, for example, the Abbot Suger. He had at least two clients, God and the King of France, and he combined his religious and political campaigns in a single building project. After supervising the construction of the Abbey Church of St. Denis, he wrote about it to make sure that everyone got the right message.

Suger began rebuilding St. Denis in 1124. He treated his writings as an integral part of the project of which he was patron and architect. His two little books on St. Denis are testimonies to the abbot as well as to the abbey church. Erwin Panofsky's brilliant study of Suger centers on the mixture of motives behind his project: defense against detractors; personal vanity; awareness of the novelty of the church's style and of its distinctive aesthetic qualities; and the consequent need both to record and to justify these assertions of art.

Suger's writings present his aesthetic and organizational enthusiasm to us as piety and zeal in the service of God. But they also betray his delight and pride. The complexity of tone these motives sometimes produce is evident in the first consecration stanza:

> Further we ordered the year of the consecration, lest it be forgotten, to be inscribed in copper-gilt letters in the following manner:
>
> "For the splendor of the church that has fostered and exalted him,
> Suger has labored for the splendor of the church.
> Giving thee a share of what is thine, O Martyr Denis,
> He prays to thee to pray that he may obtain a share of Paradise.
> The year was the One Thousand, One Hundred, and Fortieth
> Year of the Word when [this structure] was consecrated."

The verses on the door, further, are these:

> "Whoever thou art, if thou seekest to extol the glory of these
> doors,

Marvel not at the gold and the expense but at the craftsmanship
of the work.
Bright is the noble work; but, being nobly bright the work
Should brighten the minds, so that they may travel through the
true lights,
To the True Light where Christ is the true door.
In what manner it be inherent in this world the golden door
defines:
The dull mind rises to truth through that which is material
And, in seeing this light, is resurrected from its former
submersion."

And on the lintel:

"Receive, O stern Judge, the prayers of Thy Suger;
Grant that I be mercifully numbered among Thy own sheep."[12]

As Panofsky notes, there is a play on *decus ecclesiae* ("splendor of the church") in the first two lines. The first incidence refers to the spiritual honor of the institution (or to its *decus*—leader, founder, patron—fused with that honor). The second refers to the physical beauty of the church.[13]

All this is amiable and disarming, the playfulness of someone who doesn't take himself too seriously, and it accords with the tenor of the inscription as a whole. Yet the stanza is primarily a piece of self-memorializing centered on a dialogue, an exchange, between Suger and the patron saint. A self-aggrandizing countermessage thus fights with the first message for control of the statement. And in lines 3 and 4, "giving thee a share," Suger's witty verbal echoes of *participans/participem* and *orat/exores* impose a donee's obligation on the saint.

Panofsky describes Suger's process of "self-affirmation through self-effacement," and notes the difference between

> the Renaissance man's thirst for fame and Suger's colossal but, in a sense, profoundly humble vanity. The great man of the Renaissance asserted his personality centripetally, so to speak: he swallowed up the world that surrounded him until his whole environment had been absorbed by his own self. Suger asserted his personality centrifugally: he projected his ego into the world that surrounded him until his whole self had been absorbed by his environment.[14]

This doesn't seem quite right to me. I would prefer to say, first, that he projected his ego into the art and structures—political as well as architectural—by which he surrounded himself, and second, that his project of self-affirmation through self-effacement is always skewed by the assertive manner in which he affirms his self-effacement.

What causes the tensions quickening Suger's prose is the commitment to art. It is not only that the City of Man and its technical accomplishments can't be entirely left behind by the Christian striving for humility and nearness to God. Such Christians as Suger don't want to leave it so far behind that they have to deny themselves the pleasure and pride of their works in art. In Suger's prose the tones of self-confidence and thankful devotion, pride and careful humility, childlike delight and self-conscious qualification of the delight—these sound together or separately, replace each other, fuse, and often clash. His awareness of his own contribution—his creative energy fusing the roles of organizer, builder, patron, and allegorist—is everywhere apparent, and so there is all the more reason for his counterassertions of the power of God.

We're not in the position to decide whether the Suger behind his writing was sincere, or hypocritical, or self-deceiving. Whether or not he suffered twinges of "guilt," he was aware of the existence and attitudes of detractors: His work displays a need to justify his aggressive commitment to art. St. Bernard was at first his chief critic, but if we glance briefly at Bernard's rhetoric in the following passage, we'll see that he had his own problems.

The prologue to St. Bernard's treatise on the four degrees of love—*De diligendo deo,* written in the 1120s—illustrates his complex self-awareness:

PRAEFATIO

Viro illustri domino Haimerico, ecclesiae Romanae diacono cardinali et cancellario, Bernardus abbas dictus de ClaraValle, Domino vivere, et in Domino mori.

Orationes a me, et non quaestiones poscere solebatis: et quidem ego ad neutrum idoneum me esse confido. Verum illud indicit professio, etsi non ita conversatio: ad hoc vero (ut verum fatear) ea mihi deesse video, quae maxime necessaria viderentur, diligentiam et ingenium. Placet tamen, fateor, quod pro carnalibus spiritualia repetitis, si sane apud locupletiorem id facere libuisset. Quia vero doctis et indoctis pariter in istiusmodi excusandi mos est; nec facile scitur, quae vere ex imperitia, quaeve ex verecundia excusatio prodeat, si non injuncti operis obeditio probat: accipite de mea paupertate quod habeo, ne tacendo philosophus puter. Nec tamen ad omni spondeo me responsurum. Ad id solum quod de diligendo Deo quaeritis, respondebo quod ipse dabit. Hoc enim et sapit dulcius, et tractatur securius, et auditur utilius. Reliqua diligentioribus reservate.[15]

PREFACE

To the illustrious lord Aimeric, cardinal deacon and chancellor of the Roman Church, Bernard, called abbot of Clairvaux, life unto the Lord and death in the Lord.

You were wont to ask prayers from me, and not the solution of questions; and, indeed, I feel myself sufficient for neither. The former, it is true, my profession imposes, even if my conversation does not; but for the latter (to speak sooth) methinks I lack what seem chiefly necessary, diligence and understanding. Nevertheless it pleases

> me, I confess, that you seek spiritual things in return for carnal, although it were surely better to have done so from one more rich than I. But since it is the custom of learned and unlearned alike to make excuses of this kind, and it is not easy to know whether the excuse proceeds truly from incompetence or from modesty, unless the performance of the work enjoined shows, accept out of my poverty what I have, lest by keeping silence I should pass for a philosopher. I do not, however, promise to answer all; to that alone which you ask concerning the love of God, I will make what reply He will give. Keep the rest for the more diligent.[16]

Self-assertion and ironic self-deprecation both press into the rhetoric. Striking an attitude, he points to himself striking an attitude. Claiming poverty, he reminds us of the pride that lurks in such claims. His pleas of inadequacy betray, as he knows, his pleasure in rhetoric: *locupletiorem* here means not only richer in substance, whether spiritual or material goods (literally, it means place-rich and can thus connote status). It also means richer in words. His approval of the addressee's motive—seeking spiritual things in return for carnal (some favor done Bernard by the Cardinal Aimeric?)—flashes a mordant reminder of the inequity of the exchange and of the misdirection of the request. The cardinal should have appealed directly to Christ, a richer source, for the power to confront such questions himself.

Bernard's edginess is aimed chiefly at his own performance. Nothing he can do will suffice at this point; both speech and silence betray the thrust of self. The impression is that of a speaker painfully constricted by self-consciousness, and this dramatizes the first degree of love, *amor carnalis*, by which a man loves himself for himself before all other things. The opening lines of the work proper, which follow this prefatory passage, convey the effect of a leap beyond self-constriction:

> You would hear from me, then, why and how God is to be loved?
>
> I answer: The cause of loving God is God; the manner is to love without measure. Is this enough?

> Vultis ergo a me audire, quare, et quomodo diligendus sit Deus? Et ego: Causa diligendi Deum, Deus est; modus, sine modo diligere. Estne hoc satis?

But the leap is broken; the tone is terse, a touch irritable (more so in the Latin). That answer is enough for the wise; but he will have to go into it more deeply for those who are slower.

According to Panofsky and Meyer Schapiro, Bernard disapproved of art "not because he did not feel its charms but because he felt them too keenly," and his conflicted feelings are finely registered in his rhetorical style, which gives play to the very sensuous richness he condemns in religious carvings.[17] Moving back to Abbot Suger, we can see similar twists and turns in self-expression, but they take a different form because of their relation to his architectural project. In the following passages he analyzes the relationships of the creative act in order to affirm the priority of God's contribution over man's.

> But the rear panel, of marvelous workmanship and lavish sumptuousness . . . we ennobled with chased relief work equally admirable for its form as for its material, so that certain people might be able to say: The workmanship surpassed the material.[18]

> Thus, when—out of my delight in the beauty of the house of God—the loveliness of the many-colored gems has called me away from external cares, and worthy meditation has induced me to reflect, transferring that which is material to that which is immaterial, on the diversity of the sacred virtues: then it seems to me that I see myself dwelling, as it were, in some strange region of the universe which neither exists entirely in the slime of the earth nor entirely in the purity of Heaven; and that, by the grace of God, I can be transported from this inferior to that higher world in an anagogical manner.[19]

> If golden pouring vessels, golden vials, golden little mortars used to serve, by the word of God or the command of the Prophet, to

> collect the blood of goats or calves or the red heifer: how much more must golden vessels, precious stones, and whatever is most valued among all created things, be laid out, with continual reverence and full devotion, for the reception of the blood of Christ! Surely neither we nor our possessions suffice for this service. If, by a new creation, our substance were reformed from that of the holy Cherubim and Seraphim, it would still offer an insufficient and unworthy service for so great and so ineffable a victim; and yet we have so great a propitiation for our sins. The detractors also object that a saintly mind, a pure heart, a faithful intention ought to suffice for this sacred function; and we, too, explicitly and especially affirm that it is these that principally matter. [But] we profess that we must do homage also through the outward ornaments of sacred vessels, and to nothing in the world in an equal degree as to the service of the Holy Sacrifice, with all inner purity and with all outward splendor. For it behooves us most becomingly to serve Our Saviour in all things in a universal way and without any exception; Who has fused our nature with His into one admirable individuality; Who, setting us on His right hand, has promised us in truth to possess His kingdom; our Lord Who liveth and reigneth for ever and ever.[20]

The materials God has made and men have polished are radiant in themselves, but the workmanship surpassed the material owing to the skill, the plan, and the spirit of one of God's poor sheep and his artisans. The workmanship is surpassed by its product because, through God's intervention, the labors of art produce more than an artifact—not merely a building but a sacred space sacramentally endowed by God with symbolic potency, the perception of which will brighten the minds of beholders. Our endeavors of art are begun and fulfilled within an encompassing aura of transcendent power. So the care and consummate art we devote to designing and assembling stained-glass windows would be fruitless if God didn't daily respond by brightening our art with sunlight.

Suger reinforces his normative message by the conventional device of echoing scriptural and sacred authorities. For example, Panofsky observes of the second passage above ("Unde, cum ex dilectione decoris domus Dei aliquando multicolor") that it is principally a quotation from John the Scot, who had translated and commented on the works of the patron saint of the abbey. The words refer with some precision both to the consecrated edifice, which is earthly slime transformed to a model of the spiritual universe, and to that universe itself.

But this normative message is challenged by a counterstatement that betrays a different view of these issues. Remember that *decus ecclesiae* refers both to the glory of an institution and to the splendor of a building. Normatively, the building embodies the institution as an image embodies a higher reality, and not only embodies it but contributes to its welfare. Normatively, Suger can legitimize his unique new style of architecture by assimilating it to the traditional and authorized images of mystical reality—for example, the theophanies of Denis the Areopagite and John the Scot. But in fact, the language of the theophanies is a necessary counterpoise to the conspicuous novelty of Suger's project, and a counterpoise to the pride in human art that his project radiates.

Panofsky shows how Suger turns his sources against themselves to justify the primarily aesthetic motivation behind his adornment of the church. The opening lines of the passage directly above, for example, echo phrases from Hebrews in which St. Paul "had likened the blood of Christ to that of sacrificial animals mentioned in the Old Testament (but solely in order to illustrate the superiority of spiritual over merely magical sanctification): Suger concludes from this comparison that Christian chalices should be more gorgeous than Jewish vials and pouring vessels." Elsewhere, in quoting the following phrase from Ephesians, "in Whom all the building groweth unto one holy temple in the Lord," he qualifies the word "building" by the parenthesis "whether spiritual or material," thereby twisting St. Paul's metaphor into a justification of super-resplendent architecture.[21]

Dionysius and John the Scot built no churches. They embodied their theophanies in words. They didn't subject them to the overbearing imagery of architectural form—overbearing because the architectural organization of space is proximate, massive, and functional, and because attention is preempted by the artifact not only in its aesthetic but also in its practical immediacy.

Clearly the artifact preempted Suger's attention. The building was more important and real to him than any of the anagogical parallels he applied to it. Their basis in metaphor was close to the surface. And in this countermessage the lines of force move in a direction contrary to the one featured in his normative message.

Our sense of the invisible is likely to conform to our sense of the visible. Suger's words, "de materialibus ad immaterialia transferendo" ("transferring from material to immaterial things"), imply this with a precision that is odd, since they reverse the normative direction of transfer. But if we construe *transferendo* in its rhetorical sense, the words literally describe metaphor, and this, added to the qualifying force of *quasi* ("as it were"), presses on the final word, *transferri*, to diminish the transcendent import of "*anagogico more.*" Remetaphorizing inadvertently takes the initiative away from demetaphorizing and threatens to fictionalize reality.

Suger's was a new style of architecture backed by a new scale of patronage and organization, and connected with an incipient nationalistic spirit. He claimed for it the status of an image manifesting a traditional vision of spiritual reality. Because traditionalness was itself an authoritative source of transcendence, it is logical that the compelling power of the new image should rub off on the spiritual referent in a manner that changes its meaning or subtly erodes its transcendence.

The physical location of Suger's inscriptions would enhance the picturing or pictorializing quality of their language and diminish the conventional or syntactic relation of words to referents. His references to the true lights, to the golden door of the building, and to the *decus ecclesiae* as architecture, would encourage identification of the anagoge with its material image. Not that this would in fact happen, of course, given only one such project. I'm merely indicating a structural possibility inherent in the situation. But the development of Gothic—with its imperious technology, its art, and its claims to encyclopedic embodiment of Christian time and space and doctrine—went far toward actualizing that possibility. It thus intensified the conflict between the values of the traditional attitude and the means of expressing them.

There is a spatial form and image even more commanding than a cathedral: a cosmos. Because humans ascribed the spherical cosmos they invented to God, they were freer to reconstruct it according to their needs from the late eleventh century on. The decision to commit the Christian vision to that objective and putatively scientific model of reality suited the traditional impulse to legitimize human creations by embedding them in nature. This continued the development of what we now know to have been one of the more radical acts of pure fictive construction in Western history, all the easier to validate in that it was a cosmic error handed down from antiquity. It didn't have to be run through the demetaphorizing machine. It was simply expropriated from Aristotle.

The fiction that the cosmos wasn't a fiction may not have been traditional Christianity's only fiction, but it was one fiction too many. Copernicus found it aesthetically unsatisfying. Galileo speculated that nature, unlike Aristotle, might not abhor a vacuum. Calvin scratching the dirt under his feet was unable to find Hell where the traditional Church told him it was. Too much reality, too much transcendence, too much demetaphorizing had been packed into what was doomed to fall into the abyss of fiction.

And what, finally, about the most obvious and interesting victim—or triumph—of the demetaphorizing impulse? Was the nonfictiveness of his poem Dante's only fiction? Making the same distinction Aquinas did between theology and poetry, he claimed with a certain arrogance that his was an allegory of theologians, not of poets, and Charles Singleton found it puzzling that critics insisted on reading the *Commedia* as an allegory of poets in which the first or literal meaning of the poem is "only a fiction devised to express a second meaning."[22]

It isn't easy for us today to conceive of a self-proclaimed fictional work as having a story, a "first meaning," that denotes a real historical event. Historical locale and characters don't transform a novel into history. They make it a historical novel, a contained fictional world. Novelists don't ask us to believe. They ask us to make believe. But Dante doesn't ask us not to believe that this is God's universe and the world of the afterlife. He asks us to believe that it is. Yet if we translate his instructions into modern terms, we may find that our interpretive assumptions have more in common with theological than with poetic allegory.

The *Commedia* is a poem that fixes the reader's attention on its literary and rhetorical effects and on the way it organizes, articulates, and dramatizes its story.[23] It demands that the reader interpret the story by staying within it, not by translating and sacrificing it to other levels. Structurally, there is perfect congruence between our modern sense of the appropriate attitude toward fiction and Dante's sense of the appropriate attitude toward divine history and spiritual autobiography. He presents the *Commedia* as theological allegory because it is crucial to him that it not be viewed as a mere fiction. He can only play God by claiming not to play God, but he makes this claim as a poet on behalf of his fiction and not merely as a theologian.

If we translate his instructions into their modern equivalents we discover that the locale of each canticle is skewed by the structure of allusion in a slightly different direction from the others with respect to reality and fiction. That is, Hell seems most fictive because it is dominated by a pastiche of classical fantasies. Hell is the archaic product of the collective pagan imagination, and the pagans could not help lying because, like metaphor, they were deficient in truth.

The art of Hell is an art of ancient caricature. To be in Hell is to be lost forever in the delusions, the distortions, of the past.

Robert Durling has argued that Hell is a projection of the body of Satan—upside-down and inside-out—with its head, the actual figure of Satan, frozen in its anus.[24] Durling stresses the familiarity of this idea in Christian theology, but I would like to stress the unfamiliarity it takes on when transferred to Dante's fictive allegory of theologians. It adds to our sense of Hell as a child's palace of horrors. And especially from the Malacoda cantos on, there is much that is conspicuously ingenious and outlandish, so that we sometimes lose sense of the reality of evil. The spiritual torment, the inner pain and distortion of self, the privation of good: These are trivialized by being pictorialized.

It might seem that when evil is inscribed in physical imagery and in the flesh of the damned, it has been literalized. And we could also expect the physical punishment to provide metonymies for spiritual punishment. But here the physicality is too grotesque and the literalization too violent. The morbid delight in its description is too gratuitous.[25] Dante the author dramatizes the pressure of the infernal climate on Dante the speaker as well as on Dante the pilgrim. The credibility of the classically inspired infernal vision diminishes. We resist his subjugation of spiritual to physical and visible evil. Paradoxically, its excess of literalness makes it metaphoric because he shears away its metonymic relation to spiritual and invisible evil. We're impelled to affirm its obverse and to contradict the reduction of Hell to a freak show. Thus we insist, along with Dante the author, on the perversely metaphoric character and the fictiveness of the vision of evil.[26]

Purgatory differs in quality because it is modeled on the terraced hills of Florence. Movement through it is movement into and beyond the present actuality of life and work in the human community. The purgatorial world is nature improved by art. Human art collaborates with God to pave and plant the future. But the setting of Paradise is not a human artifact. Though the appearance of souls and other objects in the spheres is a kind of command theatrical performance, the setting itself is scientific reality in that it's the product of God's art alone. Thus the locale of each canticle is presented as less fictive, less artificial, and more real, than its predecessor.

In this manner the poem dramatizes the process of demetaphorizing; at first lost in fictiveness, it gradually overcomes its questionable origins and transcends its human maker by leading itself (and us) back to God. This, at any rate, is its plan. Its fiction is not that it isn't a fiction, but that it begins in fiction and aspires to facticity. It comprehends the whole universe both anagogically and literally within the small compass of a poem to which Dante's name is affixed. He unites what St. Augustine discreetly kept asunder. He weds his spiritual autobiography to his history of the world through the priestly offices of the medieval cosmos in a sacrament of art. According to John Freccero, his art authorizes its claim to transcendental revelation by presenting itself as "an imitation of God's book" and as "an objective commitment to the cosmic order": "The pilgrim's motion is not only a rotation around the interior object of his desire, but also . . . a revolution around the spiritual center of the universe."[27] God at both centers guarantees the metonymic energy and integrity of the wayfarer's double turning.

But does an art that imitates scripture compete with scripture? Does the exacting and immensely complex play of figures woven into the *terza rima* direct attention to its own generativity? "Does the order of language reflect the order of reality," Freccero asks, "or is 'transcendent reality' simply a projection of language? What we had always taken to be a problem of Dante criticism turns out to be the central epistemological problem of all interpretation."[28]

Freccero explores this problem during a remarkable analysis of the poem's terza rima. He notes that although Dante doubtless "believed that his verse pattern reflected some transcendent reality, . . . a contemporary skeptic might claim that the verse pattern is constitutive of that imagined reality."[29] A few pages later, he leans in the skeptic's direction: "The theological principles that seem to underlie Dante's formal pattern are themselves in turn derived from literary principles. . . . If it is possible to see in Dante's literary form a reflection of his theological beliefs, then it is equally possible to see in that theology the projection of literary form."[30] Freccero goes on to express this relation in a comparison whose form privileges the projective (or constructivist) over the reflective (or mimetic) alternative: "Just as meter gave a pattern and a regularity to the otherwise open-ended flow of our words, so God's providential intent gave meaning to the flow of time. History itself might be said to be God's poem," that is, Dante's God models the flow of history on the flow of the *Commedia's* poetry and meter.[31]

A similar interest in questions revolving around the problematic relations between fiction and facticity appears in the account of Dante's *theologia ludens* elaborated by Giuseppe Mazzotta. He shows how the potentially fictive—and disruptive—effect of the metaphors of play and art used in *Paradiso* is inhibited by a cultural tendency to elevate the aesthetic to a category of the real. Beauty "is a transcendent category," and "the universe—for the theologians and the church fathers alike—is an implicit aesthetic construction built with mathematical rigor."[32] What would it take to make it explicit—that is, to make explicit the constructedness that redefines the aesthetic as a category of the fictional?

Dante skirts this danger when he challenges theological tradition by showing "that the essence of divinity . . . can be grasped through art": "As beauty translates . . . an essence into an appearance, it actually displaces the essence into the imaginary."[33] This statement implies that beauty transforms the imaginary into the vehicle of the real and thus defictionalizes it. But the statement can also mean that beauty *fictionalizes* the essence, and Mazzotta dwells on Dante's "insight into the dangerousness of aesthetics."[34] Although Beatrice's warning against appearances in *Paradiso* 29 "does not quite confront" their "radical inconsistency" or the way they "hollow out" the substances they represent, such a confrontation is writ large in the fictiveness of *Inferno*. Its spectacles and sports reveal not only the "illusory constitution of the world" but also "the persistent presence of a supernatural reality, albeit in its demonic shape."[35]

In the concluding chapter I'll illustrate the representation of this process in a well-known passage from Shakespeare. The passage was once interpreted as a defense of medieval metonymies. I argue that it actually illustrates the process by which metonymies get remetaphorized.

ELEVEN

Ulysses as Modernist: From Metonymy to Metaphor in Shakespeare's *Troilus and Cressida*

The passage occurs in act 1, scene 3 of Shakespeare's *Troilus and Cressida.* Agamemnon and Nestor have been trying to shore up the courage of the other Greek leaders with the argument that their inability to take Troy after seven years derives from Jove's wish to test their constancy. Ulysses begs them to let him air his own view of the matter, and this leads to the following exchange:

> AGAMEMNON. Speak, Prince of Ithaca; and be't of less expect
> That matter needless, of importless burden,
> Divide thy lips than we are confident,
> When rank Thersites opes his mastic jaws,
> We shall hear music, wit, and oracle.
> ULYSSES. Troy, yet upon his basis, had been down,
> And the great Hector's sword had lacked a master,
> But for these instances.
> The specialty of rule hath been neglected;

And look, how many Grecian tents do stand
Hollow upon this plain, so many hollow factions.
When that the general is not like the hive
To whom the foragers shall all repair,
What honey is expected? Degree being vizarded,
Th' unworthiest shows as fairly in the mask.
The heavens themselves, the planets, and this centre
Observe degree, priority, and place,
Insisture, course, proportion, season, form,
Office, and custom, in all line of order.
And therefore is the glorious planet Sol
In noble eminence enthroned and sphered
Amidst the other; whose med'cinable eye
Corrects the influence of evil planets,
And posts, like the commandment of a king,
Sans check to good and bad. But when the planets
In evil mixture to disorder wander,
What plagues, and what portents, what mutiny,
What raging of the sea, shaking of earth,
Commotion in the winds, frights, changes, horrors,
Divert and crack, rend and deracinate
The unity and married calm of states
Quite from their fixture? O, when degree is shaked,
Which is the ladder of all high designs,
The enterprise is sick. How could communities,
Degrees in schools, and brotherhoods in cities,
Peaceful commerce from dividable shores,
The primogenity and due of birth,
Prerogative of age, crowns, sceptres, laurels,
But by degree, stand in authentic place?
Take but degree away, untune that string,
And hark what discord follows. Each thing meets

In mere oppugnancy. The bounded waters
Should lift their bosoms higher than the shores
And make a sop of all this solid globe;
Strength should be lord of imbecility,
And the rude son should strike his father dead;
Force should be right, or rather right and wrong,
Between whose endless jar justice resides,
Should lose their names, and so should justice too;
Then everything include itself in power,
Power into will, will into appetite.
And appetite, an universal wolf,
So doubly seconded with will and power,
Must make perforce an universal prey
And last eat up himself. Great Agamemnon,
This chaos, when degree is suffocate,
Follows the choking.
And this neglection of degree it is
That by a pace goes backward with a purpose
It hath to climb. The general's disdained
By him one step below, he by the next,
That next by him beneath: so every step,
Exampled by the first pace that is sick
Of his superior, grows to an envious fever
Of pale and bloodless emulation:
And 'tis this fever that keeps Troy on foot,
Not her own sinews. To end a tale of length,
Troy in our weakness stands, not in her strength.
NESTOR. Most wisely hath Ulysses here discovered
The fever whereof all our power is sick.

In The *Elizabethan World Picture,* E. M. W. Tillyard used Ulysses's speech to support the view that "the Tudors had inserted themselves into the constitution of the medieval universe." For him, Shakespeare testified no less than Aquinas to "the resolution to find correspondences everywhere," which was "a large part of the great medieval striving after unity."[1] As Tillyard saw it, Ulysses's speech is a farrago of commonplaces promoting a vision of order in which security and value, rights and duties, depend on criteria of position and contiguity in the vertical ranges of a hierarchic universe. God's moral order is perceptibly embodied in the spatial order of the physical world and reflected in the political order of the human world.

The passage can be construed along quasi-deterministic lines: Natural disorders produce social disorders; planetary commotion and political commotion, in other words, are related by metonymy, not by metaphor. Degree is objective rational concord, "the ladder of all high designs," and personified appetite is the objective source of discord. The bounded waters flooding the world and the son striking his father dead are only superficially terms in a metaphoric coupling. As instances of a class, or particulars in a single universe, they are related by metonymy. This Tudor call to obedience invokes the traditional order of the medieval monocosm. The harmony of spheres and correspondences manifests the integrating power that shapes the complex order of God's creation in its cosmic and historical dimensions.

Apart from the fact that the order Ulysses describes is noticeable primarily by its irrelevance and absence, there are dramatic and rhetorical problems with Tillyard's reading of the speech. Dramatically, this is one of Shakespeare's great comic scenes. Agamemnon, Ulysses, and Nestor bestride the stage as a crew of epic high-talkers competing with each other in heroic periphrases. Shakespeare represents them as conscious of their traditional literary roles and as trying to live up to the stereotypes they have become. But he also depicts them as vaguely uneasy about the exposure to which their theatrical existence subjects them. Nestor, still stretching out his life, was, as Ulysses implies, born old—"hatched in silver" (1.3.65). He continues—as Ulysses also implies—to be the voice, or rather the windbag, of experience. He dodders over his offer to meet Hector in single combat, and knits Greekish ears to his experienced tongue with a strong "bond of air."

The characters constantly jockey for rhetorical priority and place. As Agamemnon's words illustrate, their speeches abound in the nervous metacommunicative maneuvers by which they try to outface each other. Tillyard's advocate of order, Ulysses, spends much of his time slandering his comrades to their faces and plotting behind their backs. The last ten lines of his "tale of length"—as he calls it, no doubt with a certain satisfaction—are all that the situation requires. Their message is that no one has any respect for Agamemnon. Ulysses seems to have won this round, because Nestor is reduced to a two-line response, followed by Agamemnon's impatient and brusque question: "The nature of the sickness found, Ulysses, / What is the remedy?" Ulysses's remedy consists of another long speech describing how the fools Achilles and Patroclus ridicule the fools Nestor and Agamemnon.

The rhetorical dimension of the speech offers a more serious challenge to Tillyard's reading. We should be put on our guard by a peculiar pull between geocentric and heliocentric pressures in the imagery, between the earthy object at the center and the light-giving subject in the middle of the order. A closer glance at the passage beginning with "Degree being vizarded" (83) will suggest an alternative to Tillyard's medieval world.

As a "medicinable eye" (91), the sun actively orders things by providing light, performing operations on what it sees, and making its objects better than they are. This may have the positive effect of keeping order by controlling the influence of evil planets; since what they are in themselves is less important than what they do to and for others, making them keep up appearances has some practical value. But to correct the external aspects of evil objects may also be to mask (vizard) their true quality. This has a qualifying aftereffect on our sense or memory of "observe" in line 86.

In terms of the traditional reading, the heavens, planets, and earth observe degree, priority, place, and so forth, simply in the sense of fulfilling assigned roles and functions. But that's a very long "and so forth," a careful observance, a superflux of proprieties. And "to observe" often means "to conform to" or "to comply with" in a neutral, constrained, or negative sense: to pay lip service in merely formal celebration; to do what has to be done though it does not agree with your nature, as when you subordinate private will to public weal; or to mask your true intentions in order to get what you want from the Noble Eminence.

To observe degree may be to wear a vizard for the sake of hiding suspect motives or other "frailties that suffer in exposure," as Banquo puts it in *Macbeth* (2.3.126–27). Degree being a vizard, the worthiest and unworthiest show alike, or not at all. How many of the planets in the sun king's court hide evil intentions behind their observance? Why shouldn't the king grow apprehensive? His emanations of power intensify from "medicinable eye" through "corrects" to "posts like a commandment sans check."

Here, then, is a first qualification of Tillyard's thesis that the speech articulates the familiar medieval correspondence between macrocosm and body politic. The sun king's court projects a very uneasy ideal. Consider, for example, the pomp of "the glorious planet Sol / In noble eminence enthroned and sphered." We know why the Tudors and their successors were nervous—why, if they were "th' observ'd of all observers," they were also the observers of all the observant, posting medicinable spies throughout the kingdom.[2] For "no man is the lord of anything . . . till he communicate his parts to others"—"as when his virtues aiming upon others / Heat them, and they retort that heat again / To the first giver" (3.3.115–17, 100–102).

The royal planet is not the metonymic double of a human ruler. It is a metaphor, an ideological fiction, a hyperbole by which the apprehensive ruler exalts his theatrical display of power to the skies. Solar observance has the quality of a masque or pageant. If this is meant to offer a model of the kind of propaganda a successful ruler needs, it betrays at the same time the precariousness, the anxiety, that motivates the propaganda. For degree is not only a circling dance but a "ladder of all high designs," and these designs emanate not only from on high but from within the envious hearts of the climbers goaded upward by *philotimia*.

By the end of the passage appetite rather than order has become the basic reality. "Order" is reduced to a set of artificial distinctions and constraints necessitated by that reality, and rubbing against its grain. "Degree" becomes a euphemism for the law and order by which the regime's foreign and domestic foes may be pacified. It is only through theatrical and political performance, through the ability to maintain control of the organs of pomp and power, that the ruler who plays the sun may preserve a claim to the "authentic place"—and may even preserve the authenticity of the place itself.

At line 117 we come closest to the source-image of the ruler's anxiety in what purports to be the proper situation of justice. Justice resides between the endless jar of right and wrong, and so does its embattled agent: he strains perpetually to stave off discord, and he is perpetually jarred by the mere oppugnancy that is human nature. "When degree is suffocate," the line of order between degree and chaos is paper-thin.

This leads to a second qualification of Tillyard's reading. Ulysses implies that Agamemnon's problem springs chiefly from his inability to perform like a good leader. The general is no sun king. When "degree is shaked," it suddenly seems to become more like a siege ladder than a court—an instrument of war used by the Greek general to justify his priority of place. But the general's failures in the arts of public display and intelligence-gathering have led him to be dismissed as a fool. He has mastered neither the musical lyre nor the martial bow of concord. A model king must be melodic and melliferous—not only a warrior but also a dispenser of honey. Ulysses gives Agamemnon a sample of the honey by which the general can mollify the foragers—raiders—who circle around him as around a hive. The honey is the music of the sun king's spheres, with the foragers around the hive transformed or mellified into the observers around the throne.

In this view of the speech, what may at first appear to be an innocent evocation of medieval commonplaces is eventually felt as a disenchanted, even cynical, lesson about their political deployment. The speech vibrates with the awareness that its commonplaces are more fictive than real, or if real, real only to the extent that the royal actor successfully communicates to others his parts and theirs. The human partner in the correspondence is at any rate more real than the cosmic partner. He is its creator; and the cosmic sun king's court betrays its genesis in imitating the uneasiness and interestedness of its human original.

This is not the metonymy of active correspondence between the parts of a single universe. Ulysses's imitation contradicts the basic medieval premise, which is that although nature and society are different embodiments of the cosmic order, society can and should make nature its model. His figures of speech work to deform his image of nature. They denaturalize it. His solar system is metaphorically skewed to reflect a sophisticated vision of court politics. It suggests human complexities that are unduplicatable in the natural order.

Even if we read the speech out of context, what we see is not merely that it fails to exemplify medieval thought. If anything, the speech is a parody of it, a challenge to it. For it demetonymizes this order and shows it up as a metaphoric construction. Tillyard picked out only the medieval surface of the speech. That surface rides on a more complicated and skeptical perception of order which flaunts its modern commitments by putting traditional metonymies in metaphoric scare quotes. The traditional center of this order is not so much displaced (or "decentered") as relegated to a more inert position. It becomes the ground against which the new perception articulates itself. The conditions for destroying the difference between metaphor and metonymy are established, but that difference is then recuperated as a thematically significant opposition.

In *Troilus and Cressida* the cosmos that was around Dante's poem has vanished. It survives only within his poem, and within other antique artifacts that are stranded on a foreign shore,—but not on an alien shore. We respond to Dante as we do, not so much because he is for all time, but because, in spite of himself, he is of our time. His poem is now more real than the world it refers to. The medieval Christian cosmos and experience have become as fictive as his poem. And so our disenchantment casts an infernal shadow over his art. What *Inferno* was to the pagan fantasy, *La Divina Commedia* as a whole is to the medieval fantasy. And what Dante thought he transcended returns to haunt us. Like the return of the repressed, the return of radical metaphor from ages of metonymic displacement breaks the transference. To borrow William Blake's term, God becomes Nobodaddy. The divine analyst arises to find himself a rose merely, another blossoming of poetic metaphor.

NOTES

1. TWO FIGURES: (1) METAPHOR

1. But not by Robert Burns, whose famous rose appears in a simile, and in a context that's rhetorically complex enough to raise doubt about the kind of performative work the statement does:

> O my Luve's like a red, red rose
> That's newly sprung in June.
> O my Luve's like the melodie
> That's sweetly play'd in tune!
>
> As fair thou art, my bonnie lass,
> So deep in love am I:
> And I will love thee still, my dear,
> Till a' the seas gang dry.

The first quatrain is a stagy profession that seems aimed at the world at large, but the second redirects this outburst and its staginess to his "bonnie lass" while changing from "Luve" to "love"—from a proper to a common noun and then to a verb, from dialectal to standard usage, and, momentarily, from "cute" to high-toned diction. The third and fourth quatrains return to "luve" (the verb) and "Luve" respectively. As the referent of "Luve" oscillates back and forth between his beloved and his affection, a string of glib hyperboles makes the protestation increasingly hard to accredit. By poem's end the melody has gone *desafinado*, and the term limits implied in the *carpe diem* sentiment affixed to its opening simile assert themselves.

2. Paul de Man, *Allegories of Reading: Figural Language in Rousseau, Nietzsche, Rilke, and Proust* (New Haven: Yale University Press, 1979), 65 n.10.

3. What about "my love is *the* rose"? Does this imply that the speaker's love (whether his beloved or his passion) is more precious, more valuable? Or does it simply turn off metaphoricity and assert a floral preference? I glance at these issues to remind readers of how rudimentary an analysis of this sort must be so long as it ignores tonal nuances and contextual cues, also of how such decontextualized discussions like those that follow must inevitably diminish the (admittedly familiar) tropes they consider from living to dead or half-dead metaphors.

4. "More desperate than a metaphor," the trope of catachresis, or *abusio*, "is the expressing of one matter by the name of another which is incompatible with it, and sometimes clean contrary." John Hoskins, *Directions for Speech and Style* (1599), ed. Hoyt Hudson (Princeton: Princeton University Press, 1935), 11.

5. Christine Brooke-Rose, *A Grammar of Metaphor* (London: Secker and Warburg, 1958).

6. Brooke-Rose analyzes, for example, figures that execute the metaphoric turn with nouns, verbs, and other parts of speech, also with copulative, genitive, and other types of construction.

7. The existential sense is strong in that it asserts identity: "My love exists as a rose." The predicative sense is weak in that it indicates resemblance and slackens toward mere simile: "My love has roselike qualities."

8. Reticent when compared with "*the* rose is my love." "A rose": which one?, we wonder.

9. Donald Davidson, "What Metaphors Mean," in Davidson, *Inquiries into Truth and Interpretation* (Oxford: Clarendon Press, 1984), 257–58.

10. This explanation differs in emphasis from the one given by Meyer Abrams: "A *dead metaphor* is one that, like 'the leg of the table,' is so commonly used that we are no longer aware of a distinction between the two subjects, 'leg' as the limb of an animate creature . . . and [as] one of the supports for a table" (M. H. Abrams, *A Glossary of Literary Terms* [New York: Holt, Rinehart and Winston, 1957], 37). Though I

remain aware of the distinction, I don't consider it relevant because I don't visualize a human leg attached to a table. The referent of the term has become "whatever animate and table supports have in common," that is, "support."

11. This emphasis on the "not really," the element of negation, makes my view of metaphor differ substantially from the majority of views, which focus on positive relations of similarity, as in the following statement: "The metaphor . . . takes us from one thing to another in such a way that the first casts light on the second. . . . The limitation of metaphor is that it tells us what something is like, not what it is. Similes are overt metaphors" (Ralph McInerny, *A First Glance at St. Thomas Aquinas* [Notre Dame: Notre Dame University Press, 1990], 136–37). In my view the denoted "limitation" of metaphor—its ostensive failure to identify or even assimilate the two terms it forces together—is its strength. Metaphor isn't a closet simile. Rather, it has the appearance of a collapsed simile that "casts light" by so assertively proclaiming identity between two unlike terms as to highlight the element of unlikeness. McInerny's book is admittedly a pop version of his *The Logic of Analogy: An Interpretation of St Thomas* (The Hague: Martinus Nijhoff, 1961), but the simplicity of exposition doesn't distort the conceptual analysis and makes it more perspicuous to readers unacquainted with the Thomist tradition of analogy discourse.

12. George Lakoff and Mark Johnson, *Metaphors We Live By* (Chicago: University of Chicago Press, 1980), 5.

13. Ibid.

14. The first two metaphors are discussed in Lakoff and Johnson, *Metaphors We Live By*, 4–7, the second two in George Lakoff and Mark Johnson, *Philosophy in the Flesh: The Embodied Mind and its Challenge in Western Thought* (New York: Basic Books, 1999), 60–67.

15. In *Philosophy in the Flesh*, the more ambitious and aggressively self-promoting sequel to *Metaphors We Live By*, Lakoff and Johnson shift the context in which metaphorical concepts are examined from the relatively vague "experiential" field of the "conceptual system" to the "cross-domain conceptual mapping" operations of the "cognitive unconscious" (*Philosophy*, 57–58). They define the cognitive unconscious as "all unconscious mental operations concerned with conceptual

systems, meaning, inference, and language" (12), and argue at length that these are embodied operations involving the brain's neural structures and the sensorimotor apparatus. The traditional theory they target holds that metaphor "is a matter of words, not thought," that metaphorical language is "deviant" and typically confined to "poetry, rhetorical attempts at persuasion, and scientific discovery," and that metaphors "express . . . pre-existing similarities between what words normally designate and what they designate when they are used metaphorically" (119 and 118–27).

16. George Lakoff and Mark Turner, *More Than Cool Reason: A Field Guide to Poetic Metaphor* (Chicago: University of Chicago Press, 1989), 138.

17. Ibid.

18. The distinction between dead and conventional metaphors is further articulated in Lakoff and Turner, *More Than Cool Reason*, 128–31, and in Lakoff and Johnson, *Philosophy in the Flesh*, 82, 84, 87, 119–25.

19. See Lakoff and Johnson, *Metaphors We Live By*, 13.

20. See Lakoff and Johnson, *Philosophy in the Flesh*, 64–67.

21. Lakoff and Turner, *More Than Cool Reason*, 52. "Aspects of one concept, the target, are understood in terms of nonmetaphorical aspects of another concept, the source" (59); relations, properties and knowledge in the source domain get "mapped onto" relations, properties and knowledge in the target domain (63–64). Such metaphoric mappings, or models, whether acquired experientially or culturally, "organize our knowledge" (65).

22. Lakoff and Turner, *More Than Cool Reason*, 4.

23. Lakoff and Johnson, *Philosophy in the Flesh*, 126. See also Lakoff and Turner, *More Than Cool Reason*, 126, 198, and Lakoff and Johnson, *Metaphors We Live By*, 147–55.

24. Davidson, "What Metaphors Mean," 257.

25. Nelson Goodman's characterization of metaphor is similar to theirs: "The difference between simile and metaphor is negligible. Whether the locution be 'is like' or 'is', the figure 'likens' . . . by picking out a certain common feature." *Languages of Art* (Indianapolis: Hackett, 1976), 77–78.

26. Ibid., 258. Similes are trivially true "because everything is like everything, and in endless ways" (254). Lakoff and Turner wrongly

characterize Davidson's position in order to fit it into one of their cubbyholes containing mistaken traditional views, e.g., "The meaning of a metaphorical expression can only be the literal meaning of the expression, since that is the only kind of thing there is" (*More Than Cool Reason,* 126–27; see also 218); see below, for Davidson's own qualification of this idea. They implicitly ascribe to Davidson the position that "metaphors are trivially false, though they may on occasion be trivially true" (127), but this ascription seems based on a misreading of the statement I just cited.

Lakoff and Johnson categorically reject the thesis that metaphor involves mapping at the verbal/rhetorical rather than the conceptual level, and this leads them to classify Davidson among "antimeaning theorists, who deny that metaphor has anything to do with meaning or truth" (*Philosophy in the Flesh,* 122). This is clearly a mistake on their part, probably based on such assertions by Davidson as "lying, like making a metaphor, concerns not the meaning of words but their use" (258); the assertion doesn't "mean" that metaphoric statements are devoid of meaning; it "means" that we determine what they might mean by how they are used. Although Davidson rejects theories that attribute to any metaphor "a special cognitive content," like those of Max Black and Owen Barfield, his emphasis on use and interpretation presupposes the *production* of new meaning: "We attempt to evoke *what* the metaphor brings to our attention"; we focus "on *what* the metaphor makes us notice" (262, my italics). What is the "what" in each statement if not "the unexpected or subtle parallels and analogies it is the business of metaphor to promote" (256)? "Metaphor belongs exclusively to the domain of use. It is something brought off by the imaginative employment of words and sentences" (247).

During their critique of the "myth of objectivism" in *Metaphors We Live By,* Lakoff and Johnson ascribe to Davidson the position that "if meaning is to be objective," it must be "independent of use," "context-free," and stripped of "subjective elements." They support this claim by citing Davidson's statement that "literal meaning and truth conditions can be assigned to words and sentences apart from particular contexts of use" ("What Metaphors Mean," 247; *Metaphors We Live By,* 201–2). But as the passages cited in the preceding paragraph of this note clearly indicate, the "subjective" interaction of readers with metaphors is central to Davidson's conception of metaphor (see also the closing paragraph of "What Metaphors Mean," 264). In addition, the context of the passage Lakoff and Johnson quote shows that Davidson's statement has nothing to do with objectivism. He insists "on the distinction between what words mean and what they are used to do" only in order to argue (1) that "metaphor belongs exclusively to the domain of use" but (2) that its "imaginative employment of words and sentences . . . depends entirely on the ordinary meanings of those words" and "of the sentences they comprise." "Adverting to" the literal meaning and truth conditions words have "apart from particular contexts of use" thus "has genuine explanatory power" because it enables us to foreground the particularity of different "contexts of use" (247).

2. TWO FIGURES: (2) METONYMY

1. I. A. Richards, *The Philosophy of Rhetoric* (New York: Oxford University Press, 1936), 96–97 and 96–138. Richards called the grammatical subject of a metaphor (e.g., "my love") its "tenor."

2. In Greece today, moving vans bear the name *metaphora*.

3. In an appendix to *A Grammar of Motives* (New York: Prentice-Hall, 1945), Kenneth Burke identifies metaphor, metonymy, synecdoche, and irony as "four master tropes," notes that they "shade into one another," and defines metaphor as "a device for seeing something *in terms of* something else. It brings out the thisness of a that, or the thatness of a this" (503). The same value is assigned to these tropes not only by Vico but also by the seventeenth-century Dutch rhetorician Gerardus Vossius, by Du Marsais in the early eighteenth century, and by Fontanier almost a century later. What I enumerate above as relations of metonymy, Burke ascribes to the trope of synecdoche, the "noblest" instance of which, "the perfect paradigm or prototype for all lesser usages, is found in metaphysical doctrines proclaiming the identity of microcosm and macrocosm, related as part for whole, in which either can represent the other" (508). For my purposes, as will soon become clear, it makes more sense to follow the lead of Genette, Jakobson, Metz, and others who demote synecdoche to one of the several formally distinct

relations of metonymy enumerated above. See, for example, Christian Metz, *The Imaginary Signifier: Psychoanalysis and Cinema,* trans. Celia Britton et al. (Bloomington: Indiana University Press, 1982), 177–78. Title abbreviated to *IS* in future references.

4. This definition appears not under *metonymia,* however, but under one of its synonyms, *denominatio.*

5. The trickle-down from such schematizations as those formulated in the rhetorical tradition is apparent in dictionary listings of the various modes of contiguity and association I list above: between whole and part, container and contained, sign and thing signified, material and thing made, cause and effect, genus and species.

6. In *Metaphors We Live By,* Lakoff and Johnson claim that where metaphor is primarily conceptual—"principally a way of conceiving of one thing in terms of another"—metonymy "has primarily a referential function" in that "it allows us to use one entity to stand for another" or "to refer to another that is related to it" (35–36), usually in a specific relation (part for whole, producer for product, object used for user, institution for personal agents, place for institution, etc.—and vice versa). The distinction between conceptual and referential is not crystal-clear, partly because the apparently parallel distinction between metaphoric "thing" and metonymic "entity" is opaque. Clarity isn't restored by their subsequent remark that "metonymic concepts allow us to *conceptualize* one thing by its relation to something else" (39, my italics). since that wipes out the conceptual/referential distinction. Given their restrictive theory of metaphor as conventional (i.e., weak) metaphor, or metaphoric simile, they could better fortify the distinction by emphasizing the preexisting and dynamic or motivated relation between the two terms of a metonymy. In fact, the examples of metonymy they discuss indicate that they are concerned with the signifying function Charles Sanders Peirce calls indexical. On Peirce's theory and distinctions see my *Fictions of the Pose: Rembrandt Against the Italian Renaissance* (Stanford: Stanford University Press, 2000), 20–26.

The difference between metaphor and metonymy is discussed in a similar manner but with the help of a slightly different terminology in Lakoff and Turner, *More Than Cool Reason,* 100–4.

3. MAKING METAPHORS, SEEING METONYMIES

1. See Roman Jakobson and Morris Halle, *Fundamentals of Language*, 2nd ed. rev. (1956; The Hague: Mouton, 1975), 69–96; Jakobson, *Studies on Child Language and Aphasia* (The Hague: Mouton, 1971), chaps. 4–7, especially 41–42, 51–55. Chapter 5 of the latter was published in revised form in Jakobson, *Language and Literature*, ed. Krystyna Pomorska and Stephen Rudy (Cambridge, Mass.: Harvard University Press, 1987), 95–114, and, under the title, "The Metaphoric and Metonymic Poles," in *Selected Writings*, 7 vols., vol. 2: *Word and Language* (Berlin: Mouton, 1971), 254–59. See also Christian Metz, *The Imaginary Signifier: Psychoanalysis and Cinema*, trans. Celia Britton et al. (Bloomington: Indiana University Press, 1982), 149–297, esp. 174–82. Title abbreviated to *IS* in future references.

2. For a brief summary of attempts to regroup "long lists of 'small-scale', closely defined figures" into "larger figural regions" like those of metaphor and metonymy, see Metz, *IS*, 178–79.

3. *IS*, 175, 180. Discussing this influence, Metz observes that although the ideas of difference and opposition are fundamental to the Saussurian linguistics and phonology Jakobson took his terms from, even there "the relation of opposition can . . . only arise on the basis of an underlying 'resemblance'" (181).

4. In this I follow I. A. Richards. See *The Philosophy of Rhetoric*, 125–28.

5. Claude Lévi-Strauss, *The Savage Mind* (London: Weidenfeld and Nicolson, 1966), 106; *La pensée sauvage* (Paris: Librairie Plon, 1962), 141.

6. Metz's citations of Lacan seem chosen to emphasize precisely this difference: metaphor and metonymy are represented "by two different arrangements of the signifier S and the signifier S': 'maintenance of the bar' . . . in metonymy, and 'crossing of the bar' with metaphor" (303). What "maintenance of the bar" means at a colloquial level of discourse is suggested by Metz's next quotation from *Écrits*: "What does man find in metonymy if not the power to circumvent the obstacles of social censure? Does not this form, which gives its field to truth in its very oppression, manifest a certain servitude inherent in its presentation?" (Jacques Lacan, *Écrits*, trans. Alan Sheridan [New York: Norton, 1977], 164, 158, 160). Such servitude is ironically characterized

by a statement of Lacan's that Metz quotes at the beginning of this comment: Displacement is "the most appropriate means used by the unconscious to foil censorship" (ibid.).

7. Paul Ricoeur, *La métaphore vive* (Paris: Editions du Seuil, 1975), 228–38. Umberto Eco, "The Semantics of Metaphor," in *The Role of the Reader: Explorations in the Semiotics of Texts* (Bloomington: Indiana University Press, 1979), 69.

8. See, for example, Guy Rosolato, "L'oscillation métaphor-métonymique," *Topique* 13 (1973): 75–99.

9. Edmund Leach, *Culture and Communication: The Logic by Which Symbols Are Connected* (Cambridge: Cambridge University Press, 1976), 14. We should bear in mind Metz's warning that although metonymy "presupposes contiguity . . . not all contiguities are metonymic. . . . Metonymy is a *figure* of contiguity . . . it does not happen automatically . . . it must be put into operation" (*IS*, 198).

10. Gérard Genette, *Figures of Literary Discourse*, trans. Alan Sheridan (New York: Columbia University Press, 1982), 107, 110, and passim. Genette gives a brief moderrn genealogy of this tendency in *Figures III* (Paris: Editions du Seuil, 1972), 25.

11. William Empson, *The Structure of Complex Words* (London: Chatto & Windus, 1951), 341.

12. *Webster's Dictionary of Synonyms*, 1st ed. (1942; Springfield, Mass.: G. & C. Merriam, 1951), 49.

13. Ibid., 546. Webster's discusses metonymy under its own name (along with synecdoche), but not metaphor; the reader who looks up "metaphor" is redirected to "analogy." Synecdoche is also treated as a subclass of metonymy in Lakoff and Johnson, *Metaphors We Live By*, 36.

14. Compare the following account:

> A logical person could not mean to say that John Doe is a pig; he must mean only that John is *like* a pig! True, if the term pig is used often enough to designate people who eat in excess or in some unmannerly fashion, the makers of dictionaries, recognizing a secondarily analogous term, will define it as "a person who resembles a pig." But by this time the term has ceased to have the force of the original metaphor, and . . . has become a commonplace epithet.

(George P. Klubertanz, *St. Thomas Aquinas on Analogy: A Textual Analysis and Systematic Synthesis* [Chicago: Loyola University Press, 1960], 145)

Klubertanz is critical of Thomists whose rationalizations of metaphor reduce it to epithet. But even logicians can distinguish metaphors from premises and similes and are thus capable of appreciating the superiority of "is" to "is like"—the sharper and more ironic impact the negative or counterfactual bounce of "is" gives any utterance recognized and designated as a metaphor. In this example, the negative bounce has an ethical spin ("is not" mutates quickly into "should not be") that animates the utterance even when it loses its original metaphoric force.

15. Given my commitment to and rationale for this distinction, I can't agree with the more flexible view adopted by Fernand Hallyn, who follows Michel De Coster in assigning three possible statuses to metaphor, "a *discursive* status (valid in the case that aims to enlighten or convince), a *methodological* status (implying a heuristic function), and a *theoretical* status (linked to a vision of the world that poses *a priori* the existence of a real analogy)": *The Poetic Structure of the World: Copernicus and Kepler*, trans. Donald M. Leslie (New York: Zone Books, 1990), 28. Hallyn claims that "only the two latter types belong in a poetics of the hypothesis" (ibid.). It seems to me that the discursive and methodological uses of metaphor in contexts of persuasion and pedagogy, respectively, belong together, whereas Hallyn's characterization of theoretical metaphor sets it off from the others and approximates my definition of metonymy. Hallyn goes on to criticize schemes that tend to subsume metonymy and synecdoche within the category of metaphor (29), and his subsequent discussions of metonymy avoid this conflation, largely by restricting metonymy to substitutions in the categories of contiguity and of cause and effect. See, for example, his excellent comments on "the metonomy of perception" in Copernicus's writing: "Any perception is the equivalent of a metonymy: an empirical relation or an effect (the content of the perception) always appears in the place of its cause (the state of affairs that provokes the perception)" (80–81). And any verbal account of perception that substitutes the effect for the cause ("[I see that] the sun moves around the earth") is surely based on "the

existence of a real analogy" between two empirically related sources of relative motion. See the discussion of Nietzsche's account of metonymy in chapter 4.

16. Personal correspondence.

4. METONYMY, METAPHOR, AND PERCEPTION: DE MAN AND NIETZSCHE

1. Paul de Man, *Allegories of Reading: Figural Language in Rousseau, Nietzsche, Rilke, and Proust* (New Haven: Yale University Press, 1979), 123, 106, 110, 105.

2. Ibid., 98–99; see also 102, 117, 124–25.

3. Ibid., 5–7, 14–19, 60–74. Proust's distinction between the tropes is evaluative, metaphor being credited with greater transformational power than metonymy. See, for example, the correlation of metaphor with analogy, necessity, identity, and totality, and of metonymy with contiguity and chance, illustrated by de Man in the following contrast: "The inference of identity and totality that is constitutive of metaphor is lacking in the purely relational metonymic contact: an element of truth is involved in taking Achilles for a lion but none in taking Mr. Ford for a motor car" (14).

4. Ibid., 102.

5. Ibid., 92.

6. Ibid., 91.

7. The most obvious candidate for deconstruction is the claim that Dionysian (Wagnerian) music somehow falls outside of the category of representation and escapes the "negative valorization" accorded that category. See ibid., 94–98.

8. In the compact summary de Man gives of his reading of *The Birth of Tragedy* at the end of his second Nietzsche chapter, he cites the "pseudo-historical arguments" with which Nietzsche justifies the undermining of the genetic account: "Nietzsche's auditors have to be spoken to in Dionysian terms because, unlike the Greeks, they are unable to understand the Apollonian language of figure and appearance." Nietzsche writes that for the ancients "the Dionysian was explained by the image. Now it is the image that is explained by

Dionysos. We have therefore an exactly reversed relationship." It follows, comments de Man, "that the entire system of valorization at work in *The Birth of Tragedy* can be reversed at will. The Dionysian vocabulary is used only to make the Apollonian mode that deconstructs it more intelligible to a mystified audience" (117–18).

9. Ibid., 108.

10. Ibid., 107. In Nietzsche's own words, the correlation of outside and cause with inside and effect "enters our consciousness only after it has found a language that the individual understands. . . . 'To understand', naively put, merely means: to be able to express something old and familiar" (108). For the original, see Nietzsche, *Gesammelte Werke* (Munich: Musarion Verlag, 1922), 3:805. I use the phrase, "naive consciousness," to refer to the structure Edmund Husserl characterizes as the *natural standpoint,* or *natural attitude:*

> I find continually present and standing over against me the one spatio-temporal fact-world to which I myself belong, as do all other men found in it and related in the same way to it. This "fact-world," as the world already tells us, I find to be *out there,* and also take *it just as it gives itself to me as something that exists out there.* All doubting and rejecting of the data of the natural world leaves standing *the general thesis of the natural standpoint.* "The" world is as a fact-world always there; at the most it is at odd points "other" than I supposed . . . but the "it" remains . . . a world that has its being out there. (Edmund Husserl, *Ideas,* trans. W. R. Boyce Gibson [1931; New York: Collier Books, 1962], 96)

11. De Man, *Allegories of Reading,* 107.

12. Ibid., 108. For the original passage, see *Friedrich Nietzsche on Rhetoric and Language,* ed. and trans. Sander L. Gilman, Carole Blair, and David J. Parent (New York: Oxford University Press, 1989), 24. Abbreviated *FNRL* in subsequent references.

13. *FNRL,* 23.

14. The complete title of the first is *Der letzte Philosoph. Der Philosoph. Betrachtungen über den Kampf von Kunst und Erkenntniss (The Last Philosopher. The Philosopher. Reflections on the Struggle between Art and Knowledge).* The other is *Über Wahrheit und Lüge im aussermoralischen Sinne.*

15. *FNRL,* 21. Translation of final clause slightly altered ("gives itself" replaces "presents itself": "unsere Stilistik sich als eine durch Lesen zu percipirende giebt," 20) so as to impart a Lacanian spin to the meaning. The translators' rendering of "lauten" as "public" makes good sense, although "spoken [out loud]" more sharply focuses the figuratively echoic relation of speech to prose.

16. Ibid., 25. For the distinction between tropes and rhetorical figures, see ibid., 64–83 (Lecture 8), especially 64–67.

17. My translation: "Die Kraft, welche Aristoteles Rhetorik nennt, . . . zu finden und geltend zu machen, was wirkt und Eindruck macht" (*FNRL,* 20). In his discussion of this passage, de Man notes that however "daringly paradoxical" its formulations seem, they have antecedents in Nietzsche's "so-called Romantic predecessors" and differ only in being "more categorical" and thus marking "a full reversal of the established priorities which traditionally root the authority of language in its adequation to an extralinguistic referent meaning" (*Allegories,* 106).

18. *FNRL,* 21, translation altered to strengthen the adversative force of the original.

19. "Der Reiz" bears more loaded senses that its relation to "reizen" teases it into yielding: charm, irritation, attraction, annoyance.

20. Daniel Breazeale, trans. and ed., *Philosophy and Truth: Selections from Nietzsche's Notebooks of the Early 1870s* (1979; Atlantic Highlands, N.J.: Humanities Press International, 1991), 41. See also the comments by Richard T. Gray in his edition of *Nietzsche's Unpublished Writings: From the Period of Unfashionable Observations,* vol. 11 of *The Complete Works of Friedrich Nietzsche* (Stanford: Stanford University Press, 1995), 485–88. Subsequently referred to as *UW.*

21. Gray, *UW,* 485.

22. *FNRL,* 65–67.

23. Gregory Vlastos, introduction to Plato, *Protagoras,* trans. B. Jowett, revised by Martin Ostwald (Indianapolis: Bobbs-Merrill, 1956), xxi.

24. *Philosophy and Truth,* 48–49.

25. To go beyond Nietzsche for a moment, this varies from sense to sense. Visual perception is freer of, its content more abstracted from, the physical and physiological phenomena of transmission than are aural and haptic perception. For a brilliant phenomenological analysis

of the effects of these differences on perceptual data, see Hans Jonas, *The Phenomenon of Life: Toward a Philosophical Biology* (New York: Delta Books, 1968), 135–56. For example, among the distinctions between sight and hearing Jonas picks out different levels of vibration. Light frequencies are too high to be visibly sensed as such, and since as a result visual sensations play little or no role in transmitting visual information, sight is a relatively "quiescent" form of experience. The vibrations that cause visual sensing are neutralized—retinal responses do not relay them to the brain—so that vision gives pressure-free experiences of objects In hearing, as opposed to vision, the perception of sound is a mechanical event. Unlike light frequencies, sound waves pulse slowly enough to be directly sensed as vibrations, and sound is experienced as a vector impact, that is, as coming-from-out-there-toward-us (Jonas, 136, 145–49).

26. *Philosophy and Truth*, 50–51.

27. Ibid., 84.

28. Arthur Danto, *Nietzsche as Philosopher* (New York: Macmillan, 1968), 39. Danto makes the important observation that what gets transformed consists of our experiences (*Empfindungen*) rather than of the things we experience, and he goes on to show how this distinction is the basis of a major difference between Nietzsche and Kant (39–40; see also 95–96).

29. *Aristotle's* De Anima *in the Version of William of Moerbeke and the Commentary of St. Thomas Aquinas*, trans. Kenelm Foster and Silvester Humphries (New Haven: Yale University Press, 1951), 350: "Here begins Book III in the Greek text; for the good reason, apparently, that it is here that Aristotle begins to examine the intellect."

30. *Philosophy and Truth*, 88–89.

31. *FNRL*, 25.

32. Ibid., 59.

33. In addition to *FNRL*, 25, see *Philosophy and Truth*, 48 (¶142), 49 (¶145), 52 (¶152), 58 (Appendix ¶11).

34. Friedrich Nietzsche, "On Truth and Lies in a Nonmoral Sense," 84.

35. In one short sentence packed with considerable arrogance and even more misunderstanding, Lakoff and Turner dismiss Nietzsche's

views on metaphor as an example of the misguided approach they call "The It's All Metaphor Position." See George Lakoff and Mark Turner, *More Than Cool Reason: A Field Guide to Poetic Metaphor* (Chicago: University of Chicago Press, 1989), 218, 133–35.

36. See, for example, *UW*, 75, and *FNRL*, 24–25, 58–59. On Nietzsche vs. Kant in the context of mystification and critique, see Gilles Deleuze, *Nietzsche and Philosophy*, trans. Hugh Tomlinson (New York: Columbia University Press, 1983), 73–110.

37. *UW*, 67. Nietzsche uses the same example to illustrate metaphor in *Philosophy in the Tragic Age of the Greeks*, trans. Marianne Cowan (Chicago: Henry Regnery, 1962), 41–42: When Thales announced that "not man but water is the reality of all things," he broke through the mythopoetic Greek view of nature as an anthropomorphic "disguise" or "masquerade," but unfortunately he did not "become quite sober enough to reach the pure abstraction, 'all things are one.'" Expressing "philosophic intuition . . . through scientific reflection is the only means for the philosopher to communicate what he has seen. But it is a sad means; basically a metaphoric and entirely unfaithful translation into a totally different sphere and speech. Thus Thales had seen the unity of all that is, but when he went to communicate it, he found himself talking about water!" (44–45). "['The unity of all that is,' 'the reality of all things'] is water": A is B, but not really. Thales is guilty of an unacknowledged or unconscious metaphor.

38. *UW*, 63.

39. *UW*, 75–76.

40. See p. 29 above.

5. METAPHOR, METONYMY, AND REDUNDANCY

1. Margaret Ferguson, "Saint Augustine's Region of Unlikeness: The Crossing of Exile and Language," *Georgia Review* 19 (Winter 1975): 844. A revised version of this important essay subsequently appeared in *Innovations of Antiquity*, ed. Ralph Hexter and Daniel Selden (New York: Routledge, 1992), 69–94.

2. Willard Van Orman Quine, *From a Logical Point of View*, 2nd ed. rev. (New York: Harper & Row, 1963), 22.

3. Ludwig Wittgenstein, *Philosophical Investigations,* 115, trans. G. E. M. Anscombe, 2nd ed. (Oxford: Basil Blackwell, 1958), 48e.

4. Rosalind Coward and John Ellis, *Language and Materialism: Developments in Semiology and the Theory of the Subject* (London: Routledge & Kegan, 1977), 53.

5. Max Black, *The Labyrinth of Language* (New York: Mentor Books, 1969), 22–24.

6. Ralph Berger, *Psyclosis: The Circularity of Experience* (San Francisco: W. H. Freeman, 1977), 74–75, 77–78.

7. Gregory Bateson, *Steps to an Ecology of Mind* (New York: Ballantine Books, 1972), 130–31.

8. Responding to these pages, Susan Stewart noted that "when Ray Birdwhistell used to teach this idea of Bateson's he would then say that if this redundancy is the case then why is further redundancy introduced as the recipient of the message invariably looks out the window—for confirmation? to express consent or agreement in the fact? In other words, it's not 'if' you look out the window, it's 'when' you look out the window. The implication is that metonymy only works because of a constant affirmation of belonging; all these statements and gestures and other more tacit acts of making the world go around" (personal communication). I'm very grateful to Professor Stewart for this and many other comments that helped me re-think my approach to the issues discussed here.

9. Willard Van Orman Quine, *From a Logical Point of View: 9 Logico-Philosophical Essays,* 2nd ed. rev. (New York: Harper and Row, 1961), 44.

10. Marshall Sahlins, *Culture and Practical Reason* (Chicago: University of Chicago Press, 1976), 32, 36.

11. Pierre Bourdieu, *Outline of a Theory of Practice,* trans. Richard Nice (Cambridge: Cambridge University Press, 1977), 91.

6. THE SEMIOTICS OF METAPHOR AND METONYMY: UMBERTO ECO

1. Umberto Eco, *A Theory of Semiotics* (Bloomington: Indiana University Press, 1976). 48–49; for a more analytical and leisurely statement, see 50–51.

2. Ibid., 283; see also 121–29.

3. In semiotics, the "basic or minimal unit of meaning . . . is the *seme*, and . . . two or more semes existing together in a more complex unit of meaning comprise a *sememe*" (Louise Schleiner, *Cultural Semiotics, Spenser, and the Captive Woman.* [Cranbury, N.J.: Associated University Presses, 1995], 71). Example: "In [William] Blake's poetry the following sememe could be attached to the term 'city': industrial, black, crowded, poverty, pain, evil, filth, noise" (Bronwen Martin and Felizitas Ringham, *Key Terms in Semiotics* [London: Continuum, 2006]). Each term in the list is a seme.

Borrowing Louis Hjelmslev's terminology, Eco premises that sign functions are produced through the rulebound correlation of elements of "an *expression plane*" with those of "a *content plane*" (*Theory of Semiotics,* 48). The content or sememe is composed of a network of "semes," and these are either denotative or connotative. Thus "the content of the sign-vehicle/dog/ is a given sememe « dog » as opposed to other sememes"; "certain physical properties or zoological features" are the denotative semes through which /dog/ denotes « dog, » and the seme, « fidelity, » is a connotative marker (84–85). I follow Eco's graphic conventions throughout this discussion: single slashes enclose terms or phrases intended as expressions; guillemets (« . . . ») indicate something intended as the content of an expression; single and double quotation marks are for emphasis and quotation respectively; "italic denotes terms used in a technical sense" (xi).

4. See Eco's critique of previous theories of the sign in *Semiotics and the Philosophy of Language* (Bloomington: Indiana University Press, 1984), 14–45.

5. Ibid., 162.

6. See especially *A Theory of Semiotics,* 58–59, on the referential fallacy and 60–62 and 66 on reconceiving the referent as a cultural content. For an incisive critique of the theory of the referent in Eco and Althusser, see Thomas E. Lewis, "Notes toward a Theory of the Referent," *PMLA* 94 (1979): 459–75, especially 459–66. In *Semiotics and the Philosophy of Language,* Eco casually remarks that "the main object of all of Jakobson's research is . . . language in action," or "signification," that is, sign production (170).

7. Eco, *Theory of Semiotics*, 279–83 and 122–25. See Roman Jakobson, *Studies on Child Language and Aphasia* (The Hague: Mouton, 1971), and *Language in Literature*, ed. Krystyna Pomorska and Stephen Rudy (Cambridge, Mass.: Harvard University Press, 1987). See also Roman Jakobson and Morris Halle, *Fundamentals of Language*, 2nd ed. rev. (The Hague: Mouton, 1975).

8. Eco, *Theory of Semiotics*, 280. The following passage from Eco's note on graphic conventions reveals the pressure of his careful bracketing operation: "Since this book is concerned not only with verbal signs but also with objects, images or behavior *intended as signs* [my emphasis], these phenomena must be expressed through verbal expressions: in order to distinguish, for instance, the object automobile from the word automobile, the former is written between double slashes and in italic. Therefore *//automobile//* is the object corresponding to the verbal expression /automobile/, and both refer to the content unit « automobile »" (xi). Note that the context for introducing *//automobile//* is that of extraverbal or -linguistic sign systems. What Eco puts into play by means of this procedure and calls an "object" is not the automobile as a thing in itself, a referent, but the automobile-thing as a semantic entity, a cultural signifier: "The object *//automobile//* becomes the sign-vehicle of a semantic unit which is not only « automobile » but, for example, « speed » or « convenience » or « wealth »" (28). Eco's examples of "objects" tend to be physical signals like a note on a musical scale, a red flag, a skull, pointing fingers and other kinesic indicators, and traffic lights (88–89, 114, 119–20, 234, 127–28). On the constraints involved in approaching objects as signs, see 166.

9. Ibid., 168.

10. Rewriting makes different structural demands on each set: In the first set the terms in each pair will have to be reversed—"love is a rose" and "friars are dogs of God"—because "love" and "friars" are subjects of acts of predication in which "rose" and "dogs of God" are the interpretants. This symmetry is less marked in the second set.

11. Although, as I note above, Eco emphasizes the merely expressive and therefore arbitrary source of the semic identity between *Dominicanes* and *domini canes*.

12. Umberto Eco, *The Role of the Reader: Explorations in the Semiotics of Texts* (Bloomington: Indiana University Press, 1979), 80.

13. Eco, *A Theory of Semiotics*, 112–14.

14. For a critique of the limits this imposes on the ability of semiotics to elaborate a theory of the material and historical subject, see Teresa de Lauretis, *Alice Doesn't: Feminism, Semiotics, Cinema* (Bloomington: Indiana University Press, 1984), 168–79.

15. Eco, *A Theory of Semiotics*, 289.

16. Eco, *The Role of the Reader*, 68, 79.

7. FROST AND ROSES: THE DISENCHANTMENT OF A RELUCTANT MODERNIST

1. See the short and very informative Wikipedia entry, "Rose is a rose is a rose is a rose." See also Gertrude Stein, "Sacred Emily," in *Geography and Plays* (Boston: Four Seas Company, 1922), 178–87.

2. My thanks to Marie Borroff, who explained this to me many years ago. See the marvelous essay on Frost in Professor Borroff's *Language and the Poet: Verbal Artistry in Frost, Stevens, and Moore* (Chicago: University of Chicago Press, 1979), 23–41.

8. METAPHOR AND THE ANXIETY OF FICTIVENESS: ST. AUGUSTINE

1. Charles Singleton, *"Commedia": Elements of Structure* (Cambridge, Mass.: Harvard University Press, 1965), 62.

2. For an excellent discussion of this topic and a review of the debate about it, see Teodolinda Barolini, *The Undivine Comedy: Detheologizing Dante* (Princeton: Princeton University Press, 1992), 3–20.

3. Margaret Ferguson, "Saint Augustine's Region of Unlikeness: The Crossing of Exile and Language," *Georgia Review* 19 (Winter 1975): 842. A revised version of this important essay subsequently appeared in *Innovations of Antiquity*, ed. Ralph Hexter and Daniel Selden (New York: Routledge, 1992), 69–94.

4. Kenneth Burke, *The Rhetoric of Religion: Studies in Logology* (Berkeley: University of California Press, 1970), vi.

9. METAPHOR AND METONYMY IN THE MIDDLE AGES: AQUINAS AND DANTE

1. St. Thomas Aquinas, *Summa Theologica,* Part I, Question 1, Article 10, resp.; 1.7. Translated by the Fathers of the Dominican Province in America, 3 vols. (New York: Benziger Bros., 1947).

2. Thomas S. Kuhn, *The Copernican Revolution: Planetary Astronomy in the Development of Western Thought* (New York: Random House, 1957), 25–26 and passim. The two "spheres" or "regions" are the terrestrial (sublunary) bounded by the lunar sphere and the celestial or superlunary or quintessential region containing the spheres of the planets and the fixed stars. For a compact description of this model, see A. C. Crombie, *Medieval and Early Modern Science,* 2 vols. (Garden City, Anchor Books, 1959), 1:75–76. Some versions of the model are more expansive because they include spheres for each of the four elements within the sublunary sphere. For more recent comment and revision concerning Kuhn's model, see David C. Lindberg, *The Beginnings of Western Science: The European Scientific Tradition in Philosophical, Religious, and Institutional Context, 600 B.C. to A.D. 1450* (Chicago: University of Chicago Press, 1992), 89–96 and chapters 2, 3, 9, 11, and 12 passim. See also Edward Grant, *The Foundations of Modern Science in the Middle Ages: Their Religious, Institutional, and Intellectual Contexts* (Cambridge: Cambridge University Press, 1996), 104–26 and 133–41.

3. Charles S. Singleton, trans. and comm., in Dante Alighieri, *The Divine Comedy, Paradiso: Commentary* (Princeton: Princeton University Press, 1975), 442–43. On Aristotle's notion of the *primum movens* and its relation to the *primum mobile,* see Crombie, *Medieval and Early Modern Science,* 1:77–78.

4. Dante, *The Convivio,* IV.iv, trans. Philip A. Wicksteed (London: J. M. Dent, 1903), 73–74, slightly altered. The roots of the concept of Primum Mobile are to be found in the eighth book of Aristotle's *Physics,* and they are embedded in his attempt to prove that the universe is spherical, and therefore finite, and that its rotational movement is eternal. On logical, physical, and metaphysical grounds, he postulates the necessity of an unmoved first mover, and argues that this mover must be "either at the center or at the circumference [the sphere of the fixed stars], since these are the principles. But the things nearest the

mover are those whose motion is quickest, and in this case it is the motion of the circumference that is the quickest, therefore the mover occupies the circumference": *Physics,* 267b, trans. R. P. Hardie and R. K. Gaye in *The Complete Works of Aristotle: The Revised Oxford Edition,* ed. Jonathan Barnes, 2 vols. (Princeton: Princeton University Press, 1984), 1:446. The discourse of Christian realism easily transforms this text. McInerny remarks how useful it was for Aquinas to find such "proofs for the existence of God . . . formulated by a man uninfluenced by revelation" (*First Glance at St. Thomas Aquinas,* 142).

5. Kuhn, *Copernican Revolution,* 114.

6. According to commonsense conviction, what we see is more real than the explanations we give to account for them. But how and what we see are already theory-laden, weighed down with presuppositions and de-posits. For a clear statement of the distinction between a physical or descriptive hypothesis that furnishes sufficient proof and a mathematical hypothesis that may explain but does not itself reflect the appearances it saves, see St. Thomas Aquinas, *Summa Theologica,* Part I, Question 32, Article 1, ad. 2. The descriptive hypothesis is assimilated to the real observational phenomena it is believed to verify (Aquinas's example is the proof "that celestial movements are of constant speed") while the mathematical hypothesis "is not fully conclusive since an explanation might be possible even on another hypothesis." For the probable source of this distinction in a passage quoted by the sixth-century commentator on Aristotle, Simplicius, and attributed to a certain Geminus, see Crombie, *Medieval and Early Modern Science,* 1:87–89. See also Hallyn, *Poetic Structure of the World,* 110–11: "One important consequence of the Aristotelian point of view is that mathematical astronomy is secondary to physical astronomy" because the former "must conform to the [putative] physical framework, compared to which its constructions appear increasingly hypothetical, even fictitious."

7. Those who were "largely responsible for keeping alive a knowledge of the liberal arts and classical philosophy and science in the early Middle Ages . . . follow[ed] the traditional practice of a long line of compilers and commentators who had long since lost contact with the classical originals. In many cases the late encyclopedists were removed

from classical Latin authors by five or six, and from Greek authors such as Plato and Aristotle, by ten intermediate sources. . . . Yet they give the impression that they are handling the original works. . . . Notwithstanding their shortcomings, these rudimentary compendia were to hold a central position in the intellectual development of the West for nearly a millennium." William Stahl, introduction to Macrobius, *Commentary on the Dream of Scipio,* trans. Stahl (New York: Columbia University Press, 1952), 9–10.

8. *Convivio,* 73–74.

9. Copernicus still uses this form of metonymizing animism even while engaged in a refutation of Aristotelian method: "I believe that gravity is nothing but a certain natural desire, which the divine providence of the Creator has implanted in parts." Nicholas Copernicus, *On the Revolutions,* trans. Edward Rosen (Baltimore: Johns Hopkins University Press, 1978), 18. Perhaps this usage has only the apologetic function of making the argument seem more innocuous to Church authorities by using traditional formulas—a "defensive reflex against potential detractors" (Hallyn, *Poetic Structure of the Universe,* 67).

10. St. Thomas Aquinas, *Summa Theologica,* Part I, Question 66, Article 3, ad. 4. Translation based on the bilingual text edited and translated by members of the English Dominican Province (the Blackfriars edition), *Summa Theologiae,* 60 vols. (New York: McGraw-Hill, 1964), 10:46, but altered to bring it into closer conformity with the Latin text:

> Sed quia corpus firmamenti etsi sit solidum, est tamen diaphanum, quod lumen non impedit, ut patet per hoc, quod lumen stellarum videmus non obstantibus mediis caelis, potest aliter dici quod habet lucem caelum empyreum non condensatam, ut radios emittat, sicut corpus solis, sed magis subtilem. Vel habet claritatem gloriae, quae non est conformis cum claritate naturali.

Occasionally, as above (see note 1), I have also consulted and at times used the earlier translation of the Fathers of the English Dominican Province published in America (New York: Benziger Bros., 1947), entitled *Summa Theologica,* and based on a conflation of texts clearly different from that of the Blackfriars edition.

11. On these textile connotations, see the entries under *subtilis* and *tela* in the Lewis and Short *Latin Dictionary*.

12. *Summa Theologiae*, I, 67, 1, resp. Translation altered:

> Et similiter dicendum est de nomine "luminis." Nam primo quidem est institutum ad significandum id quod facit manifestationem in sensu visus; postmodum autem extensum est ad significandum omne illud quod facit manifestationem secundum quamcumque cognitionem.
>
> Si ergo accipiatur nomen "luminis" secundum suam primam impositionem, metaphorice in spiritualibus dicitur. . . . Si autem accipiatur secumdum quod est in usu loquentium ad omnem manifestationem extensum, sic proprie in spiritualibus dicitur.

13. "In the traditional account terms (*nomina*) are of three kinds: univocal (having the same meaning in all of its uses, as *horse*); equivocal (having different meanings that have no relation to each other, as *dog* said of animal and star); and analogous (having several meanings which are partly the same and partly different or which are related to one another, as *healthy*)." Klubertanz, *St. Thomas Aquinas on Analogy*, 6.

14. James F. Anderson, *The Bond of Being: An Essay on Analogy and Existence* (St. Louis: B. Herder, 1949), 174–75.

15. See Hallyn's comments on "the production of analogous effects" in *The Poetic Structure of the World*, 27: "two non-contiguous positions, not influencing each other directly, but sustained by the same presupposition, two (or several) events 'falling' from the same point. . . . By attaching parallel events to a common presupposition to which they refer, we demonstrate that the parallels are not purely imaginary, that they are not abstract and gratuitous correspondences attributable solely to the observer."

16. Those who practiced analogical interpretation "sought to find in visible form a foothold from which to mount upwards to the *perception* of spiritual realities." M.-D. Chenu, *Nature, Man, and Society in the Twelfth Century: Essays on New Theological Perspectives in the Latin West*, trans. Jerome Taylor and Lester K. Little (Chicago: University of Chicago Press, 1968), 113, my italics. The choice of words betrays the mystified desire actually to see invisibilia.

17. Ralph M. McInerny, *The Logic of Analogy: An Interpretation of St. Thomas* (The Hague: Martinus Nijhoff, 1961), 149.

18. Walter. J. Ong, "Wit and Mystery: A Revelation in Medieval Latin Hymnody," *Speculum* 22 (1947): 324–25.

10. SACRAMENTAL ANXIETY IN THE LATE MIDDLE AGES: HUGH OF ST. VICTOR, THE ABBOT SUGER, AND DANTE

1. Hugh of St. Victor, *De Sacramentis christianae fidae,* I.i.x, in Jacques-Paul Migne, ed., *Patrologia cursus completes, Series Latina* (Paris: Apud Garnier, 1844–76), vol. 176, column 194D–195A, my italics.

2. Translation slightly altered from that of Henry Osborn Taylor, *The Medieval Mind: A History of the Development of Thought and Emotion in the Middle Ages,* 2 vols., 4th ed. (1927; Cambridge, Mass.: Harvard University Press, 1959), 2:94, my italics.

3. *Hugh of Saint Victor on the Sacraments of the Christian Faith (De Sacramentis),* trans. Roy J. Deferrari (Cambridge, Mass.: Mediaeval Academy of America, 1951), 15–16, my italics.

4. My translation and italics. For the reason that appears below, I prefer to render *ut mihi videtur* more literally than Deferrari, whose "in my opinion" is tonally too assertive.

5. Beryl Smalley, *The Study of the Bible in the Middle Ages* (Notre Dame, Ind.: University of Notre Dame Press, 1964), 86. Smalley appreciates the sophisticated and programmatic character of Hugh's treatises much more than a nineteenth-century editor who thought that Hugh was "the most credulous of the medieval mystics" (quoted by Smalley in *The Study of the Bible,* 85). For an excellent and much more recent study, see Margo E. Fassler, *Gothic Song: Victorine Sequences and Augustinian Reform in Twelfth-Century Paris* (Notre Dame: University of Notre Dame Press, 2011), 211–40.

6. Jerome Taylor, Introduction to *The Didascalicon of Hugh of St. Victor,* trans. Taylor (New York: Columbia University Press, 1961), 23.

7. Ibid., 28.

8. Ibid., 29.

9. Ibid., 28.

10. *Didascalicon* VI.iv, pp. 143–44.

11. Taylor, Introduction, 22; *In Hier. Coel.* I.i; *PL* 175, 925D.

12. Litteris etiam cupro deauratis consecrationis annum intitulari, ne oblivioni traderetur, praecepimus hoc modo:

> Ad decus ecclesiae, quae fovit et extulit illum,
> Suggerius studuit ad decus ecclesiae.
> Deque tuo tibi participans martyr Dionysi,
> Orat ut exores fore participem Paradisi.
> Annus millenus et centenus quadragenus
> Annus erat Verbi, quando sacrata fuit.

Versus etiam portarum hi sunt:

> Portarum quisquis attollere quaeris honorem,
> Aurum nec sumptus, operis mirare laborem,
> Nobile claret opus, sed opus quod nobile claret
> Clarificet mentes, ut eant per lumina vera
> Ad verum lumen, ubi Christus janua vera.
> Quale sit intus in his determinat aurea porta:
> Mens hebes ad verum per materialia surgit,
> Et demersa prius hac visa luce resurgit.

Et in superliminari:

> Suscipe vota tui, judex districte, Sugeri;
> Inter oves proprias fac me clementer haberi.

Abbot Suger, *Liber de Rebus in Administratione Sua Gestis,* 1.27, ed. and trans. Erwin Panofsky, *On the Abbey Church of St.-Denis and its Art Treasures,* 2nd. ed. by Gerda Panofsky-Soergel (Princeton: Princeton University Press, 1979), 46–49.

13. Ibid., 164.

14. Ibid., 29–30.

15. S. Bernard of Clairvaux, preface to *De diligendo Deo,* SANCTI BERNARDI ABBATIS CLARAE-VALLENSIS OPERUM TOMUS SECUNDUS, COMPLECTENS TRACTATUS MORALES, DOCTRINALES ET POLEMICOS, Column 973A.

16. *The Book of Saint Bernard on the Love of God,* trans. Edmund G. Gardiner (London: J. M. Dent, 191–[?]), 24–25.

17. Panofsky, *Abbot Suger*, 25–26; Meyer Schapiro, "On the Aesthetic Attitude in Romanesque Art," in Schapiro, *Selected Papers: Romanesque Art* (New York: George Braziller, 1977), 6–10.

18. "Ulteriorem vero tabulam miro opere sumptuque profuso . . . tam forma quam materia mirabili anaglifo opere, ut a quibusdam dici possit Materiam superabat opus, extulimus." *De Admin.*, 33; Panofsky, *Abbot Suger*, 60–63.

19. "Unde, cum ex dilectione decoris domus Dei aliquando multicolor, gemmarum speciositas ab exintrinsecis me curis devocaret, sanctarum etiam diversitatem virtutum, de materialibus ad immaterialia transferendo, honesta meditatio insistere persuaderet, videor videre me quasi sub aliqua extranea orbis terrarum plaga, quae nec tota sit in terrarum faece nec tote in coeli puritate, demorari, ab hac etiam inferiori ad illam superiorem anagogico more Deo donante posse transferri." *De Admin,*, 33; Panofsky, *Abbot Suger*, 62–65.

20. "Si libatoria aurea, si fialae aureae, et si mortariola aurea ad collectam sanguinis hircorum aut vitulorum aut vaccae ruffae, ore Dei aut prophetae jussu, deserviebant: quanto magis ad susceptionem sanguinis Jesu Christi vasa aurea, lapides preciosi, quaeque inter omnes creaturas carissima, continuo famulatu, plena devotione exponi debent. Certe nec nos nec nostra his deservire sufficimus. Si de sanctorum Cherubim et Seraphim substantia nova creatione nostra mutaretur, insufficientem tamen et indignum tantae et tam ineffabili hostiae exhiberet famulatum. Tantam tamen propi ciationem pro peccatis nostris habemus. Opponunt etiam qui derogant, debere sufficere huic amministrationi mentem sanctam, animum purum, intentionen fidelem. Et nos quidem haec interesse praecipue proprie, specialiter approbamus. In exterioribus etiam sacrorum vasorum ornamentis, nulli omnino aeque ut sancti sacrificii servitio, in omni puritate interiori, in omni nobilitate exteriori, debere famulari profitemur. In omnibus enim universaliter decentissime nos oportet deservire Redemptori nostro, qui in omnibus universaliter absque exceptione aliqua nobis providere non recusavit; qui naturae suae nostram sub uno et ammirabili individuo univit, qui nos in parte dexterae suae locans, regnum suum veraciter possidere promisit, Dominus noster qui vivit et regnat

per omnia secula seculorum." *De Admin.*, 33; Panofsky, *Abbot Suger*, 64–67.

21. Panofsky, *Abbot Suger*, 16.

22. Charles Singleton, *Dante Studies 1. Commedia: Elements of Structure* (Cambridge, Mass.: Harvard University Press, 1965), 88.

23. See now the incomparable and magnificent edition, translation, and commentary by Robert M. Durling and Ronald Martinez: *The Divine Commedia of Dante Alighieri*, vol. 1: *Inferno* (New York: Oxford University Press, 1996); vol. 2: *Purgatorio* (New York: Oxford University Press, 2004); vol. 3: *Paradiso* (New York: Oxford University Press, 2011).

24. Durling, *The Divine Commedia of Dante Alighieri*, vol. 1: *Inferno*, 554. See also Durling, "Deceit and Desire in the Belly of Hell," in *Allegory and Representation: Selected Papers from the English Institute, 1979–80*, ed. Stephen J. Greenblatt (Baltimore: Johns Hopkins University Press, 1981), 61–93.

25. On the gratuitousness of these punishments and their relation to Dante's "infernal irony," see John Freccero, *Dante: The Poetics of Conversion* (Cambridge, Mass.: Harvard University Press, 1986), 104–7.

26. Although my emphasis in this paragraph differs from Freccero's, I'm deeply indebted to his account of the conspicuously constructed character of an infernal reality in which "Divine Justice is a projection of Dante's hand." *Dante: The Poetics of Conversion.*, 105. See in general 93–109 for Freccero's development of this theme and his critique of Auerbach.

27. Freccero, *Dante: The Poetics of Conversion*, 214–15, 247, 250.

28. Ibid., 260.

29. Ibid., 264.

30. Ibid., 269.

31. Ibid., 270.

32. Giuseppe Mazzotta, *Dante's Vision and the Circle of Knowledge* (Princeton: Princeton University Press, 1993), 229.

33. Ibid., 228, 234.

34. Ibid., 237.

35. Ibid., 236.

11. ULYSSES AS MODERNIST: FROM METONYMY TO METAPHOR IN SHAKESPEARE'S *TROILUS AND CRESSIDA*

1. E. M. W. Tillyard, *The Elizabethan World Picture* (New York: Macmillan, 1944), 6, 77.
2. *Hamlet*, 3.1.153.

INDEX